# PLAY TO LEARN
# AND
# LEARN TO PLAY

## A FRESH APPROACH TO COACHING YOUNG PLAYERS
## 5-16 YEARS OF AGE

**Mick Critchell**

With contributions from
Bo Bosma, Richard Cheetham and Mark Hurst

Play to Learn - Learn to Play
by Michael Critchell

ISBN-13: 978-1-59164-181-0
ISBN-10: 1-59164-181-0

Library of Congress Control Number: 2013938305

*Art Direction and Layout*
Bryan R. Beaver

Reedswain Publishing
88 Wells Road
Spring City, PA 19475
www. reedswain.com
info@reedswain.com

# Foreword

In 1980, when I was teaching, my headmaster gave me an extra £250 to spend on the PE department, as we were building up quite a reputation for the school. I did something quite revolutionary for the time and bought three pulse meters, as I wanted to see how hard the children were working in lessons. I got a complete shock, because in some lessons, notably softball, rounders and cricket, they were often getting a higher pulse rate walking out to the field than they were in the lesson itself!

Stunned by this, we decided as a department to run a programme of all small-sided games, whether it was football, rugby, softball or cricket, with a maximum of four players on each side. For example, instead of playing softball and rounders, we devised a game which incorporated both and which provided much more action. The batting team were given four tennis balls and a tennis racket. One batsman struck the four tennis balls anywhere he chose (the only stipulation was that he couldn't play the balls behind him) and then all four batsmen had to run around the complete circuit before the fielding team recovered the four balls and placed them into a hoop. If all the batsmen got round the circuit before the fielders completed their task, then they scored a point - but nothing if the balls were returned to the hoop first. The striking team batted for 15 min and then the teams changed roles. Each team would get approximately 30 min batting and 30 min fielding each lesson.

The results were amazing. Whatever the sport, fitness levels improved dramatically. We regularly recorded pulse rates between 180 and 220 and one boy even reached 230 whilst playing cricket. However, what we were very slow to realise was that not only were fitness levels improving but so too were technical and tactical levels. For example, in our combined softball and rounders game, each player struck at least 60 to 70 balls per lesson and fielded nearly the same number. Compare this with a normal game of rounders or softball, where batsmen are lucky if they get four strikes per game. I would regard this as physical recreation not physical education! As players became more proficient at striking the ball, they then started to think about tactics. Did they hit all four balls to one fielder, so that player had trouble getting them back to the hoop or did they spread the balls around so that nobody could wait at the hoop? Similarly, the fielders had to choose whether to leave somebody at the hoop or cover the spaces on the field.

So many positive things came from what we had observed in 1981 that, from this point on, we used small-sided games as the base for teaching all invasion and striking games in school. When I was forced to retire from teaching in 1997, through injury, I was still preaching the use of small-sided games but now wanted proof that what I was saying was correct. With time on my hands, I started to research the brain and child development and quickly came to realise just how closely the two were linked. I was helped in this project by the arrival of Jark and Bo Bosma, who brought their sons along to my training sessions at The Football Garage. Jark is a consultant neurosurgeon and his wife a neuropsychologist, so if there was anything I didn't understand they were able to explain and enlighten me.

I started by analysing the game of football, which is an open-skilled game where the player has to process a huge amount of different information to achieve a maximum output (maximum output = best coordinated response combining all aspects of the game). In later chapters we will explain that the brain is a very important asset that needs to be stimulated at the highest level to be most effective.

The best way to encourage players to develop their football is by training them in such a way that the whole brain is involved and that all parts of the brain are stimulated. It is a mistake to think that analysis of all aspects of the game is the basis of all training. It is mainly the technical part of the football game that requires analysis. This relies mainly on functions initiated by the left hemisphere. Training should in fact be focussed on elements initiated by the right side of the brain - such as visual perception and movement – and the frontal lobes which are responsible for decision-making.

The most effective training, therefore, is by playing small-sided games. Every player has to be involved, has a large number of touches, and has to make a lot of decisions about movement off and on the ball and about which skills to use. In this way, we stimulate the right as well as the left side of the brain at the highest brain level (cortex).

Especially at younger ages, it is necessary to play smaller games to stimulate and optimise the higher cortical functions and memory functions. If the amount of information that the player has to process overrides the memory capacity, then learning will be ineffective and the training is likely to be counterproductive. The information the player must process increases as we put more players on in the game. Unfortunately this is what usually happens in training at grass-root as well as professional level!

Football poses a tremendous challenge to coaches because it is a game of constant motion where instant decisions have to be made in ever-changing situations. Therefore, the coaching system has to be carefully structured to create a learning environment that enables all players to reach their full potential. Bo, Richard, Mark and I all agree that small-sided games, which promote whole brain thinking, are the best way to achieve this. Young players must be given the freedom to play, experiment, take risks, improvise and make mistakes. By intelligently introducing the appropriate coaching methods at the right time, players will become confident of making decisions by themselves. This book uses a progressive system of small-sided games which enables players to find their own way.

Finding out how players learn has enabled us to understand how best to coach. We hope this book will help bring about change - because change needs to happen if we are to produce players with creativity and flair and who can adapt to ever-changing situations. Only then will we be able to compete with the best.

These are ideas that I have collated over many years and I feel reassured that someone as highly regarded as José Portolés, renowned expert, Spanish football coach and professor, endorses my approach to coaching and supports the view that an understanding of neuroscience can help coaches and young player development.

**Michael Critchell**
*November 2011*

Mick delivering to the Polish Football Association, Warsaw, April 2010

# How an understanding of neuroscience can help coaches and young player development

*José V. Portolés Montañés*

To speak about football is easy, and very common. To speak about "football player development" is easy too, and everyone thinks it is easy to teach football. We watch games on TV or at a stadium and then we get our children to replicate the professionals; my friend Mark in England talks about "Match of the Day Managers". But to actually speak about "football learning" with a high level of quality is neither easy nor common.

To be in charge of a young team or group of beginners we need to know less about football and more about the "child as a human being". Science has to be seen as important for improving our knowledge and our interventions with beginners. If we understand our children as individual "human beings", who are completely different from adults, we will accept that it is necessary to know in depth what they are like and how to teach them in order to create the best learning environment for them.

The motor learning process, as the base of player development, is the main subject we need to master when we work at youth level. So, we have to know about areas such as motor behaviour evolution, the motor control of actions, the effects of each exercise or practice stimulation, the applied methodology, the pedagogical principles, the relationship between emotional state and performance and many others factors that enhance young player quality development.

During the past 30 years we have come to know more about the brain than ever before in human history, but we don't know everything about brain function yet. In fact, we only know a fraction. The important brain feature is called "plasticity" and the process "context dependent". It is determined by our daily activity and the stimuli we face every moment, every second of our lives. The good news is that we can select the processes which generate the best stimuli in order to create a "rich context" in which we can provide the best conditions for improving in any human area. Thus, it is very important to select the correct pedagogical actions in order to influence and direct the "plasticity process". For example, if we use a "military methodological-context" we will have a better chance of developing "coach-dependent" players who are reproductive, disciplined etc, but we cannot hope to develop creative, tactically intelligent, independent thinking and self-regulating players.

As coaches we need to know the "specific behaviour" of our children and which are the main aspects that allow us to create the correct context for generating the best learning process. The new research in neuroscience, together with pedagogical principles and methodological techniques, are the best tools we have to ensure we are giving to children what they need to develop their full potential.

When we understand the close relationship between the cortex and the limbic system, we can understand better the strong link between the emotional level and the cognitive one. The links between thinking, believing, feeling and motor behaviour are systemic and so strong that the failure of one of them will seriously affect the others. Then performance and development will not be as good they could be. It is argued that "football is not a science". Possibly - but I want see science as a tool for better understanding about what I do, because the children and players deserve to be respected and get the best from me, so it is my responsibility and my obligation to be better each day to help them develop.

But what about "the game", you ask, as this book is about football?  But the child should always be first, and never the reverse. When we use football as play, we are giving the main importance to "enjoyment", but if we use football as a means (ie how do we win this match?) we are detracting from the play essence. We have to build a culture of 'football for children', not adults, and never put the children second to the football. This is one important reason for knowing more about children's behaviour and development. We must never forget "the adults are the offspring of childhood", not vice versa.

Mike has understood perfectly the difference and he has been able to create a book that shows the importance of being rigorous in arguments and, very importantly, a book that is easy to read and understand. Mike's current book will certainly help me to improve, just as it will help you too. Many thanks, Mike.

©José V. Portolés Montañés
Borriol, 18-04-2012

# Acknowledgements

I would like to thank my good friends Mark, Bo and Richard for giving up their time to write three extremely important chapters for this book. The regular chats and conversations over the phone were invaluable and a constant source of inspiration. Also, Steve Tribe for the graphics, IT support and professional input, without which the project would probably not have got off the ground. Finally, thanks to my wife Carol for her proof reading skills, patience and unequivocal support, without which I would have floundered badly.
*Michael Critchell*

I would like to thank Mick for giving me the opportunity to contribute to this book. I consider him an extremely talented football coach, who is always searching for ways to improve football training for players at grassroots and professional levels. I would also like to thank my husband; he was always willing to discuss my developing theories and when I was lost he could find the correct English words for my ideas.
*Bo Bosma*

I would like to thank Mick for asking me to contribute to the writing of this book. He has been a good friend and mentor for many years. I regard it as a privilege to have been a part of this work. I would also like to thank my partner Nicky for her unwavering support and patience throughout all my new ventures, as well as our daughter Kitty who continues to learn something every day and shows us proud parents that teaching can be done from a distance!
*Richard Cheetham MSc*

Fifteen years ago I met 'Critch' and immediately knew that I had found a kindred spirit; we were both 'failing' our FA conversion course by refusing to put down answers that we knew were out of date and wrong! We said we would write a book together one day and I'm thankful for the opportunity to contribute to this one. Since then we have worked together and bounced ideas and I learn something every time we speak. I must thank Gary Wilcox and the boys of Sandhurst Saracens, Eddie Cross and the members of the PE department at TASIS, The American School in England, who support my abstract ideas and actually bring them to life, Fernando Roig Neugroles and the Villarreal Academy and Geoff Noonan, Sean Reed and the Fulham Academy. Finally to Paula, Christian, Jack and Maureen who at times must think they come second to football and teaching research ….. you don't!
*Mark Hurst*

# Contents

| **Christian** | **Ricardo** | **Amro** | **Toby** |
| British | Mexican | Egyptian | Nigerian |

"You can discover more about a person in an hour of play, than in a year of conversation."

- Plato

**Chapter 1**

# Introduction – Future of Football and Players

Pelé's autobiography was entitled "My Life and the Beautiful Game". The association of the words 'beautiful game' with football has stood the test of time but how can this still remain if attention is not paid to the nurturing and development of players of the future? Has evolution been evident in the coaching required to prepare these young players for the changes in the modern game? The pressure on time and space evident at the highest level requires emphasis on decision-making developed on the training pitch. This must go hand in hand with attention to speed, agility and reaction time. Consequently, player development - if attended to correctly - safeguards the future of precious youthful enthusiasm alongside the adherence to mental and physical skills.

Wayne Harrison, in his book "Recognizing the Moment to Play" (*Reedswain 2003*) focuses on 'recognizing the moment' in reference to the need to optimise anticipation in game settings among defenders. This is one of the essential ingredients in football coaching and yet how often is this embedded into a training session? It is the belief of those involved in the writing of this book that there needs to be a radical re-think about the basic principles on which young players are coached, especially during their early introduction to the game where fundamental movement patterns and skills should be at the heart of any progressive programme. There is a phrase used among track and field athletes which runs "same training, same results". Investing in the old methods, where repetitive exercises or 'drills' form the basis of the coaching sessions, seems absurd as they do not provide the learning environment required to develop the skills mentioned earlier. The challenges (and the basis of this book) are to focus on matching the game requirements for players with the coaching setting and fully acknowledge the developmental role that coaches play. When researching for this book, a poignant and relevant quote from the German football coach and author, Horst Wein, was found. He stated:

*"The soccer of the past we have to respect, the soccer of today we must study and the soccer of the future we should anticipate."*

From the outset, the planning of this book was to anticipate and discuss the future of football for players and coaches. Dominic Fifield (*The Guardian, 2006*) referred to 'flawed coaching' in England, where emphasis at academy level was away from technical development and more on competitive games. There was a need, however, for greater emphasis on "more time in a training environment learning technique". Competition is less likely to hone these skills. David Pleat, interviewed for the article, commented: "English players want to play but they don't want to practise". It would be easy to blame the players, but maybe the training they have experienced lacks stimulation, relevance and appeal.

Unfortunately, coaches today are faced with problems that have not existed previously, as the children in front of them at training have grown up in completely different conditions. Sport England (2005) has referred to the 'fearful society' that restricts them from 'spontaneous play' and exploration. These activities are  commonly associated with the past. Their upbringing more often than not occurs in an urban environment devoid of open spaces and more full of risk. The environment in which children now play has been transformed from nature to concrete jungle and they are increasingly cut off from the chance to roam.  One of the greater concerns has been referred to by Professor Neil Postman in his book The Extinction of Childhood (1992). He highlights the removal of the 'normality of childhood' through an increasingly restricted and sedentary upbringing where the elements of discovery are facilitated through the use of computers and the media rather than the healthy active outdoors where cognitive and physical skills are honed.  In today's society, once children have learnt to walk, they are less required to continue to learn a broader range of movement activities that will help build a rich repertoire of motor skills. The likelihood of producing children with basic athleticism is far reduced. The youth of the future could be the first in history to grow up without experiencing natural play. As a result we are missing the 'natural athletes' who learnt to play in the streets and backyards, climb trees and go places under their own steam. These are the challenges of the modern coach and it is development of this athleticism and these motor skills that is now a task assigned to them. The world of football has not escaped these changes and remains as vulnerable as other sports.

Television (the 'thief of time') and computers have, in many developed countries, led to a generation of children deemed physically illiterate - lacking in simple movement patterns that were once taken for granted. In previous generations children would spend their free time practising with a ball. They learnt to play as individuals or as part of a team and, by continuously playing the game, learnt how to find space within the chaos of a match. They learnt by seeing and doing and by trial and error, and their understanding of the game developed naturally from this. Most importantly, they organised their own games - in the street, on fields, in back yards, on waste land, in car parks, around trees, in disused buildings and so on. They made up their own rules, depending on the space available, obstacles in the way and number of players involved. This spontaneity seems to be less apparent as Horst Wein discusses - "children are obliged to train and compete like adults" - sessions high in organisation and low in self expression and discovery.

At the same time, our children are competing against African and South American youngsters, who are more robust as a result of their lifestyle and adept in more physically demanding settings. The game of Fusball emerged from the slums of Rio set in areas lacking in that challenging "time and space" environment as discussed earlier. Fewer players, more touches, more learning, fewer errors, greater skills and more benefit! The variety of surfaces used for games are commonly played on barefoot, subsequently improving proprioception and balance. These children learn from circumstance, not from the more structured and organised training methods experienced closer to home, which fail to stimulate single abilities sufficiently for them to develop. African and South American methods develop individual play, and only when this has been achieved do they worry about team play.

The challenge for the coach is to place children in an environment that allows them to experience football in a way that is physically, intellectually and socially age-appropriate. In simple terms, the coach's job is to bring street soccer into their controlled environment. Young players need lots of uninterrupted play, which allows them to experience football at first hand. They must be given the opportunity to experiment and allowed the freedom to use their minds and imagination to adapt to the situation at hand. Allowing young players to experiment will also give them the opportunity to succeed or fail. The long-term goal is for the coach to develop a player who can recognise and solve the problems of the game.

The fact that too often children are put in a team environment, for which they are not ready, is not their fault! To coach young players effectively, coaches must have an understanding of child development and need to see players as individuals who react, develop and learn in different ways and at different speeds. Most importantly, the child must not be inundated with instructions, such as when to pass and dribble, what position to hold, who to pass to and which player to mark. Is there not a case, therefore, for recognising in effective game play and training that players are allowed to be responsible for solving problems and responding appropriately with skills and decisions as Souza and Oslin (2008) point out. This is more likely to facilitate creativity and strengthen cognitive skills.

Many clubs and coaches inadvertently foster an environment of fear, where players fear failure, fear humiliation and fear the disapproval of their peers. Players are not allowed to learn from their mistakes; instead they learn to avoid embarrassment by not trying things. This culture of fear not only destroys a player's love of the game, it also suppresses individual expression and imagination and makes them afraid to take chances. Being prepared to take chances is essential for true learning, but too many coaches promote an environment in which young players are afraid of being wrong. And yet it is through making mistakes as much as from success that learning takes place. Who could argue with one of the greatest sporting icons of the twentieth century, Michael Jordan, when he referred back to his career?

*"I've missed more than 9000 shots in my career: I've lost almost 300 games. 26 times I've been trusted to take the game-winning shot and missed. I've failed over and over again in my life. And that is why I succeed."*

The old adage was that coaches need players but players do not need coaches. Due to social change, things are different now and the coach is the most important person in an organised training session. Football therefore needs great coaches, as great coaches can produce great players. People are only transformed if they are engaged in what they are doing. It is not enough for a coach to know his discipline; he must also understand that football coaching works on relationships, feelings and motivation as well. Personal qualities such as honesty, empathy, organisation and communication, as well as knowledge, are essential if we want to raise standards and engage the children of the present and the future.

## Chapter 2

# The Fulham Investigation
**Mark Hurst**

It has long been our belief that small-sided games provide players with more time in possession of the ball and therefore more decision-making and technical development opportunities. However, we wanted proof that this was true, so we carried out a series of experiments with the support of Fulham Football Club. We wanted to look at the number of receptions of the ball and the number of actual touches after receiving the ball to determine the opportunities for technical and game intelligence development and for decision-making opportunities whilst playing small-sided games. The three players involved in the study were from the Fulham FC Academy and were chosen from the under-11 age group. Although the boys were of the same chronological age, we purposely chose three players of different biological ages. Player 1 was a 'late maturer', player 2 of 'average maturity' for the age and player 3 an 'early maturer'. Biologically there was approximately three years' difference between player 1 and player 3.

Below is a list of the conditions for the games employed in the research:

- The players played 3v3, 4v4 games without goalkeepers and 5v5, 11v11 games with goalkeepers.
- All the games were of 10 min continuous duration played on grass.
- Pitch sizes were altered according to the game and the number of players.
- In the 3v3 and 4v4 games, both teams attacked and defended two mini-goals.
- Two mini-goals were placed at each end of the pitch as corner goals.
- Spare balls were on the side of the pitch to ensure play was continuous if a ball went out of play.
- The three players wore Polar heart rate transmitters and wrist computers to record heart rates.
- Each game was filmed from above (parental consent was given).
- The three players used for the study wore brightly coloured fluorescent hats for easy identification on film for analysis purposes.
- Each of the three players was assigned a coach, who counted the number of ball receptions and number of touches the player had in each of the games. This was cross-checked with the film.
- The same three players at each club were used throughout the experiment.

| Match Size | 3 v 3 | 4 v 4 | 5 v 5 | 6 v 6 |
|---|---|---|---|---|
| Pitch Size | 15m x 18m | 20m x 22m | 30m x 25m | 100m x 60m |

Following the research at Fulham, we decided to repeat the experiment with an English grassroots club, Sandhurst Town Boys and Girls FC U11 Saracens team, managed by Gary Wilcox, and with a Spanish team of similar age. In Spain, we were fortunate enough to be able to use the Villarreal CF Academy equivalent age group, thanks to Fernado Roig Neugroles, the Director General and founder of the famed Academy at Villarreal. The conditions were identical for all three projects, although a bit warmer in Spain! Interestingly, we had to receive permission from the Villarreal Academy Director to play 11v11 ("why do you need to prove what common sense tells us?") and at U11 Sandhurst Town Saracens had elected to decline the opportunity to move to 11-a-side to play 7-a-side for as long as possible.

## FULHAM

| Match Size 3v3 | Ball Receptions | Touches | Total Touches | Average Heart Rate |
|---|---|---|---|---|
| | | | | |
| Player 1 | 36 | 51 | 87 | 188 |
| Player 2 | 35 | 52 | 87 | 186 |
| Player 3 | 37 | 54 | 91 | 184 |

| Match Size 4v4 | Ball Receptions | Touches | Total Touches | Average Heart Rate |
|---|---|---|---|---|
| | | | | |
| Player 1 | 24 | 19 | 43 | 177 |
| Player 2 | 25 | 49 | 74 | 194 |
| Player 3 | 27 | 43 | 70 | 178 |

| Match Size 5v5 | Ball Receptions | Touches | Total Touches | Average Heart Rate |
|---|---|---|---|---|
| | | | | |
| Player 1 | 18 | 25 | 43 | 191 |
| Player 2 | 26 | 43 | 69 | 188 |
| Player 3 | 22 | 35 | 57 | 178 |

| Match Size 11v11 | Ball Receptions | Touches | Total Touches | Average Heart Rate |
|---|---|---|---|---|
| | | | | |
| Player 1 | 1 | 4 | 5 | 193 |
| Player 2 | 11 | 12 | 23 | 191 |
| Player 3 | 3 | 8 | 11 | 216 |

## VILLARREAL

| Match Size 3v3 | Ball Receptions | Touches | Total Touches | Average Heart Rate |
|---|---|---|---|---|
| | | | | |
| Player 1 | 21 | 59 | 80 | 180 |
| Player 2 | 23 | 48 | 71 | 170 |
| Player 3 | 23 | 52 | 75 | 175 |

| Match Size 4v4 | Ball Receptions | Touches | Total Touches | Average Heart Rate |
|---|---|---|---|---|
| | | | | |
| Player 1 | 15 | 50 | 65 | 178 |
| Player 2 | 17 | 57 | 74 | 152 |
| Player 3 | 13 | 54 | 67 | 152 |

| Match Size 5v5 | Ball Receptions | Touches | Total Touches | Average Heart Rate |
|---|---|---|---|---|
| | | | | |
| Player 1 | 15 | 60 | 75 | 185 |
| Player 2 | 20 | 35 | 55 | 187 |
| Player 3 | 16 | 48 | 64 | 163 |

| Match Size 11v11 | Ball Receptions | Touches | Total Touches | Average Heart Rate |
|---|---|---|---|---|
| | | | | |
| Player 1 | 5 | 13 | 18 | 172 |
| Player 2 | 9 | 20 | 29 | 179 |
| Player 3 | 7 | 18 | 25 | 185 |

## SANDHURST

| Match Size 3v3 | Ball Receptions | Touches | Total Touches | Average Heart Rate |
|---|---|---|---|---|
| | | | | |
| Player 1 | 33 | 67 | 100 | 190 |
| Player 2 | 29 | 56 | 85 | 177 |
| Player 3 | 31 | 48 | 79 | 181 |

| Match Size 4v4 | Ball Receptions | Touches | Total Touches | Average Heart Rate |
|---|---|---|---|---|
| | | | | |
| Player 1 | 26 | 48 | 74 | 182 |
| Player 2 | 24 | 41 | 65 | 179 |
| Player 3 | 18 | 31 | 49 | 173 |

| Match Size 5v5 | Ball Receptions | Touches | Total Touches | Average Heart Rate |
|---|---|---|---|---|
| | | | | |
| Player 1 | 24 | 41 | 65 | 184 |
| Player 2 | 19 | 37 | 56 | 176 |
| Player 3 | 14 | 23 | 37 | 164 |

| Match Size 11v11 | Ball Receptions | Touches | Total Touches | Average Heart Rate |
|---|---|---|---|---|
| | | | | |
| Player 1 | 1 | 1 | 2 | 194 |
| Player 2 | 7 | 13 | 20 | 183 |
| Player 3 | 3 | 7 | 10 | 187 |

So what can we take from this research? Other studies, such as Fenolio's work with the Manchester United Project, comparing 4v4 with 8v8, support our findings that small-sided games give maximum opportunities for technical training. Put in quite simple terms - more opportunities to manipulate the ball in a game or practice will give greater opportunities for technical development. Contrast each player 3 in 3v3 and 11v11 with regard to total touches: 3v3 - 87, 75 and 31 and 11v11 - 11, 25 and 10. The difference is quite staggering, and yet this 11v11 on full-size pitches is what we put our 10 and 11 year olds through each Saturday and then expect them to become the technical players we cry out for at each World Cup. Many young footballers can execute technique in isolation, yet this all too easily breaks down in a game situation. Could this be because of the short term "way to win" coaching at a young age eg "get rid of it" or "get it down there", or is it because too much technical training is done in isolation away from the game itself? Add into this mix the lack of connection that young players have with each other when we put them into large- sided games too early and it is hardly surprising that in the aftermath of Euro 2012 the cry is that England are not technical enough to keep the ball, with the statistic of 32% possession proving the point. Combine these three factors and it is no surprise that we are behind in technical and game intelligence development when compared to many other areas of the world.

We still see what Drabik refers to as "military" style training, more suited to gymnastics, on the football fields of England every night, conducted by well-meaning coaches of young teams. This has to change. In terms of technique development, we cry out for good 1v1 players or creative goal scorers, but when do we give them the opportunity to develop the necessary skills? Dribbling around cones or a shooting drill with the coach with 10 in a line? Is this method conducive to providing an environment where creativity, related technical and game intelligence and fun are to the fore? We think not. Using a 4v4 game with the younger age groups, we can make the objective "score as many goals as you can". We will see lots of 1v1 skills, lots of improvisation and creativity and lots and lots of ways of scoring. Just try it and see. Stand back, don't say anything and you will be amazed how creative young players can be when they have freedom. At the same time, we will see many different ways of controlling the ball, of passing, of moving and, most of all, thousands of decisions being made. Just look at the statistics in the experiment ….. and what were we crying out for after The World Cup of 2010 and Euro 2012? (See chapter 7)

Yet technical ability alone is only one aspect of being a good football player. Game sense and movement are other areas which need to be developed if we are to improve football ability. In Chapter 3 we will explain how small-sided games, played in a random way, will stimulate and activate the whole brain. The brain learns by creating neural pathways and these develop memory templates which are used in new and future situations. If the brain is exposed to a lot of stimuli in different situations, the neural pathways and neural connections will become increasingly effective. When the network connections are growing and the memory templates are expanding, thinking and decision-making will become quicker and more advanced (ie players will be able to think ahead).

For the brain to provide good solutions, we have to **practise** making decisions. Let's look at the numbers again. If each time we are about to receive a ball we have the possibility of six decisions to make, each player in a 3v3 will have to make in the region of 200 decisions just receiving the ball. Yet in 11v11, they will have only 20 or so ….. and that is just when they receive the ball. Add to this the increased complexity of decision-making when a player has the ball, and even more so without the ball, and look again at the data. Which games provide the maximal opportunities for developing decision-making in our young players? Later in the book we will discuss the number of connections there are in each game. The level of complexity for each game is determined by the number of players on the field. Simple mathematics tells us that in 3v3 games the total number of possible interactions per team is 6, per game is 30, but for 11v11, per team the total number of interactions is 110 and per game 462 ……. at 10 or 11 years of age!! (See chapter 7)

A renowned youth coach, Juan Lu Delgado (Villarreal Academy and Valencia Academy coordinator of 5-11 year olds and currently working to develop a system of development for young players in Qatar) came to visit and we took him to watch a Premier League Academy game for eight year olds. It was 8v8 on a reduced size pitch that was still quite large. His immediate comment was that there was no connection between the players on the right-hand side of the field and the left, and that the number of players and size of pitch was forcing the players to play in one direction only …… FORWARD. Forward short or, more usually, forward long. We then watched the same club's U14s play Ajax in an 11v11 game. Ajax were complex in their movement and passing, whilst the Premier League club were simple and direct. It could be argued that the style of play at U14 was determined by the games played at eight years of age. When we spoke with the Ajax coaches, their young players had been brought up on 4v 4 from an early age and it was obvious which group of boys understood the game better, had better technique and made better decisions. Why? The reason is simple; they had practised them **in situ** for years in small-sided games. Think about it. When we teach grouping of numbers in mathematics (times-tables), we do not start with the larger complex groups 7, 9, 11, 12 etc, because the larger numbers are too complex for young developing minds and, more importantly, the larger numbers use the same patterns as the smaller numbers eg the 12 times-table is really a form of the 2-times table, 9 is 3, 10 is 5 etc and connections are made by the budding mathematicians. When your children start to read on their own, would you encourage them to read Biff and Chip or do you give them War and Peace? Which book is appropriate and why? Which book do they enjoy and why? Why don't we use the same educational logic in football with young players? (See chapters 3 and 6)

Physically, the smaller-sided games are far more appropriate. Consider the heart rates. All the games have high heart rates, but the 11v11 really is cross-country with a ball thrown in. Contrast the heart rate and involvement with the ball in the 3v3 or 7v7 against the 11v11. Are we training our young players to be better footballers or marathon runners? A German study found that 10 year olds covered 4265 metres in 25 min playing 11v11 on a full pitch. Full time Bundesliga professionals, with fully formed and highly trained energy systems, cover only 25% more ground in the same time!! What would an adult game of 30 v 30 on a pitch three times the size of a regulation pitch look like? How often would you get the ball? And, more importantly, would you want to play in such a game every week? How much fun would it be? That is what we are asking our young players to do ......AND WE EXPECT THEM TO LEARN AND IMPROVE at the same time. As the research shows, the games themselves can be the fitness/conditioning element of training, thereby giving the players more time with the ball and no need to stop the session 10 min early to do 'shuttles' or, even worse, lose 10 min at the start when they are excited about playing football to do shuttles. (See chapter 7)

The final thing that struck us from this research is that the development of young footballers can cross cultural boundaries. There is very little difference in the data between the 'élite' English and Spanish players, or between these two groups and the 'grassroots' players (though Sandhurst Saracens have been brought up on small- sided games (Villarreal style) and have never performed a drill since they were five!). 'They' don't play beautiful football because they are Spanish, Brazilian, Argentinian, African etc, but because they have been in appropriately sided games where they have had non-stop opportunities for technical development and decision-making by being at the very heart of the process rather than being bystanders in training and matches. The development is a natural progression. As José Portolés says, we don't plant a flower and then pull and stretch it to full height. We feed and water the plant, stake it when it grows tall to give it support and we patiently nurture it to blossom. (See chapter 5)

The rest of this book will look at how we can nurture all players so that they can be constantly learning, developing and improving by playing to learn. Interestingly, one of the players we used at Fulham was due to be released as he was not big enough to cope with the move to 11-a-side football. The videos showed him to be the most technical and intelligent player of all and he was retained. How tall are Spain's midfield stars? Which games did the players prefer? Over 90% of the players who took part (not just the 3s) preferred the 5-a-side. Why? Because it was more fun as they

were more involved. **They played without knowing they were learning**.
(See chapter 5)

Keith Gould who has used this method with his Sandhurst team, now
U13, contacted us to inform us that, at a recent 5-a-side tournament, they
responded to the challenge of keeping the ball by maintaining possession
for the whole of the first-half, consisting of five minutes! However, Keith's
comment is most telling: "They saw passes in the middle of the game that
we could not see on the sideline!"

*'Mini-games allow for far more successful actions, which increases self-*
*esteem – subjecting children to the traditional game only enforces failure.'*
Horst Wein

# Chapter 3

# Brain Involvement in Football Training
## (Constant, variable and random training methods)
**Bo Bosma**

In chapter 4 we will discuss the different teaching styles and which ones are more suitable to stimulate creative football, where decision-making is paramount, but in this chapter we will look at three trainings methods currently used in English football.

- Constant practice (CP)
- Variable practice (VP)
- Random practice (RP)

We are convinced that movement and game sense (also known as football intelligence/vision) are the two main components that have the highest impact on how well the game is played. Do current methods develop movement and game sense?

Before we describe the CP, VP, and RP in more detail, it is important to explain some basic cognitive development of the brain and its connection to learning. For the readers who are interested in the neurological, anatomical basis of the brain relating to learning/teaching in football, we refer to: 'Game Vision in Soccer' by Critchell, Bosma and Granger.

The brain is our computer; it regulates and affects our abilities and behaviour. Although we are born with a certain brain mass, our brain develops over the years through active input (stimulation). Our brain is built to recognise patterns and our cognitive development is considered a continuous process of assimilation of these patterns. We have to establish how we can get the best out of our brain at every stage of development.

In the embryo the brain starts to develop within four weeks of conception. The brain growth and its different functions are partly determined by our genes, but a healthy pregnancy will also benefit the positive development of the foetal brain. We are born with millions of neurons and their connections. The brain produces double the amount of neurons that we need and the ones we use will survive. As we learn/develop we will recruit more and more fibres, and establish more and more connections, thereby establishing pathways (wires) for learning. The brain action is a result of electrical impulses sent along these 'paths' of nerve fibres (wiring). The nerve fibres are wrapped in myeline (a dense fat that is like electrical tape). The myeline is an insulation of the neurons and their synapses. The more myeline, the more insulation, the faster the stimulus travels. Practice will thicken the myeline and results in a better performance.

As we grow into childhood the brain makes and breaks connections at a very high speed. The brain is very flexible and a lot of the learning that took place before we came into the world is extended. After three to four months we see activity in the cerebral cortex, the part of the brain that provides the highest cognitive function that is ultimately responsible for perception, movement and decision-making. The Frontal Lobes (FL) are the most recently developed part of the brain; they become active between the age of six months and one year. They make up about one third of the mass of the cerebral hemisphere, and they play a very large role in human behaviour, especially in the regulation of complex activities.

At approximately 11 years of age (girls) and 14 years of age (boys) the brain volume is at its highest point. It is important to realise that at this age puberty sets in and a lot of connections in the brain will change under the influence of hormones and body growth. Hence, just at the point where the brain and its pathways of learning appeared to be established, the brain will change all over again. In puberty, the wiring and rewiring of our neural pathways takes place at a very high rate. During this time a lot of functions will deteriorate, children get clumsy and their motor control recedes. They get 'slow' and their balance and accuracy will be affected. This is all due to structural changes in the brain. Connections between neural pathways get 'pruned' and, in particular, the unused neural connections give way to more stable surviving connections. It is because these unused wires are cut out that there is more space available for the development of more specialised neural pathways. This 'pruning' will make sure that the speed of electrical impulses over the remaining pathways will increase.

It is important to know that the last area in the brain to develop is the pre-frontal cortex. This is located at the very front of the Frontal Lobe. It is this part of the brain where 'intentions' are formed and it is this part that is involved in decision-making and judgement. The "teen age" is the time where a lot of new experiences and new learning take place. At this age decision-making abilities are still forming and develop all the time. The process of extending brain function will continue until the person is around 21/22 years of age. All these carefully developed cognitive functions will start to deteriorate again from our late 20s, early 30s. The complex functions which developed last will be the first to deteriorate! In our early 30s we will see slowing down in the processing of information and the working memory is slowly less able to store information. If we continue to believe that decision-making (anticipation, judgement, creativity) is essential for optimal football performance, **then no final judgement can be made about a player's ultimate level of game sense until this age!!**

In top level football, it will be these factors that determine the difference between players. If we assume that players at the highest level all have a high standard of athleticism, technical ability, speed and strength, the discriminative factor will be the cognitive contribution of the individual. The players with a high speed of thought, who have the right accurate movement patterns and the most effective decision-making, will be the best (team) players.

## Constant Practice

Constant Practice is the most basic practice method. It is based on young children's urge to imitate the things/skills around them. The practice offered in this way aims to create automatic behaviour. In football, this means that the players work alone against a wall or in pairs and repeatedly pass the ball in a complete, controlled way. They will practise the same skill over and over again. You can call this Stimulus > Response learning. This kind of learning will result in automatic skills, where the player does not have to think any more about what his foot is doing. The higher cognitive brain switches off. Constant Practice should result in a very good technical ability, but does it?

Football is an open-skilled sport (as opposed to a closed-skilled sport such as golf or snooker) where players rely on the movement and decisions of others. Therefore the game should be learned as a whole; it should not be broken down into individual, small sections of the game. Constant Practice is not in keeping with the essence of an open-skilled sport.

**FOOTBALL = GAME SENSE + MOVEMENT + TECHNICAL ABILITY**
(cortex) (cortex) (non-cortex)
Higher brain function    Higher brain function    Lower brain function

Technical ability is **part** of the game. We know that a skill is improved by repetition, simply because we operate a pathway (wire) for the muscle memory. Children will kick all sorts of balls around, but also stones, socks, pillows etc. They are 'training' their most basic motor skills this way, but in doing so, they create automatic skill learning that is controlled by the cerebellum, not by the highest cognitive brain part, the cortex. This repetitive kicking, together with other ball skills, is something children do without realising it is useful for the game. _Thus in CP we create a learning situation where there is no involvement of the highest cortical zones of the brain._

Football training must be meaningful for the player for it to be registered in the brain. Then what is learned can be called upon in a later situation where a similar response is required. Therefore, technical ability must be introduced in the framework of training where different situations are offered to the players.

In the pre-control movement stage, where the player is a complete novice and is not yet able to repeat movements in succession, learning should not be in a constant situation either. Technical learning should also be put in a situation that relates to the game as closely as possible. Kicking a ball over the same distance with no variation in space and angle will rarely be reproduced in a game situation. It does not require any decision-making or creativity (and therefore is meaningless). Obviously, the very young player should get the technical training presented in a suitable way for his age, but still in a game situation (e.g. 1v1, 2v2, 3v3).

There will be random situations present at game level that can impede your 'really nice' skill that is trained under constant conditions. Constant Practice should be used as a tool to work on aspects of football other than the ball: feet quickness, speed-running technique etc. On its own it will never be sufficient to improve the player's game in a direct way. Clearly, the repeated application of automated skills in different situations will contribute to improvement of the player's game. There is no point in spending much time on CP in an organised (team) football training session.

Research and observation have found that CP can bring about short-term changes in performance, but it is not the optimal way of training and it does not stimulate long-term learning. No effective pathways and networks will develop in CP.

Where pure technical skills should become an automatic pattern, organised by the lower brain levels, the cortex is not involved. The decision on what skill to use and when to use it in the game is part of the decision-making process and therefore has higher brain level (cortex) involvement. Making such decisions on what skills to use and when (kick left/right foot, use head etc.) is not an automatic behaviour and should therefore be trained in situations similar to the game.

## Variable Practice
In Variable Practice the player will be tested much more. The coach will focus on one skill but in a wider adaptable situation. The football tasks will involve more variation in space, time and angles, and also more players are involved. Overall, the training situation will reflect more what happens during a match. With more players in the training area and the ball moving

over a greater distance in space at variable speed, it creates a situation in which more is required of the brain.

More variable aspects determine more decision-making and therefore more meaningful learning. Also, more movement is involved and, with that, different perceptual skills are needed. For example, it is no longer enough to use only your central vision as one does in Constant Practice. The player must use his peripheral vision to keep informed about the aspects on the pitch that will influence what he does *on or off the ball*. On a primitive level, patterns are introduced and, with that, visual scanning, anticipation and creativity become part of your game play.

Although in Variable Practice we see a better analogy of the real football situation, the designated area/skill is still set by the coach. It still doesn't allow the player to use his brain in full. Set conditions prevent a player becoming creative; they prevent him from learning at the highest cognitive level.

## Random Practice

With Random Practice, technical skills, game-sense, movement and visual perception are practised at the same time. Training sessions will resemble very closely the 'real thing' e.g. the match.

You need to train the skills that are required in the game because that is the way the brain will learn. The brain learns by developing networks and creating neural pathways. It does so by myelinisation of neurons (nerves) which will increase the speed of signal transfer. This means quicker thinking and quicker decision-making.

Since Random Practice is directly related to the game, it develops the patterns and pathways for movement and game-sense much better than Constant or Variable Practice. It consists of identifying important elements and grouping them into a meaningful framework or chunk. If players are faced with different scenarios, a lot of these chunks will be recalled and built upon by combining them with new chunks or patterns created in the training game. With increasing game experience, more memory templates will be created from which the player can choose in later situations.

The creation of these memory patterns will be influenced by the cognitive ability of the player. This ability can only improve by exposing the player to a lot of game variation at a complex, random level. You need to develop mechanisms that monitor, compare and integrate all intermodal perception (input from all senses) for a maximum output to be achieved.

In simple terms: the more random the training and the more you make the aspects work together, the better you learn. The best way to do this is to be experiencing a previously known stimulus but experiencing it in a novel, random way at all times. Only then will the cortex of the brain be involved and the learning meaningful, with new assimilated and integrated brain patterns made.

Visual ability (e.g. spatial perception) and memory (processing) are the two most important cognitive skills you have to train to be able to identify all crucial elements that will help to develop these brain patterns. Information processing is a cognitive ability that has to develop with age and experience. It is with wider experience and age that players create diverse strategies to encode, process and recall information. The 'size' of the memory will increase, so more items of information can be stored. Also, in time, children get more efficient at processing the given information; this increased efficiency means that there will be more 'free' memory capacity to be used for processing even more information. Hence it is crucial for young players to play (very) small-sided games, where they have enough memory capacity to actually learn from their football experience. If the input overrides the memory capacity, then learning will not be as effective. Small-sided games will allow each child to be more involved, make more decisions, and have their foot on the ball more often. Thus, we should not play 11v11 until 13/14 years of age at the earliest.

By visual ability, we mean the need for good spatial perception. The player needs to be able to position himself on the pitch in relation to all other players and, of course, in relation to the ball. Peripheral vision is important for this. Distance (timing), space and angles are the basic spatial elements a player needs to relate to. It is this perception that makes him decide about his own movement on the field. Since the visual memory stores objects in relation to each other, the technical movements of other players will be part of the visual perception. Players who are extremely skilled at judging all these factors in the correct frame are the players who can anticipate where the space is going to be and what movement the other players have to make for him to be optimal on or off the ball. This is where game-sense and movement come together. This is why they need to be trained together so the cerebral cortex (brain) has optimal involvement. We know that playing small-sided random games stimulate and activate the whole brain at cortical (highest functional) level and both the left and right hemispheres are involved. We know that each hemisphere has its own specific ways of receiving and processing the input it gets. The left hemisphere will initiate the analysis of information: by this we mean the breaking down of information on actions (skills) into small components. Technical skills, for example, require analysis and will develop with the 'help' of the left hemisphere. The right hemisphere processes input synthetically i.e. interprets it as 'global' information; this predominantly concerns visual perception, movement and space. Therefore it 'sees' the combined information of input such as angles, distance, speed etc.

In England, most football training is based on analysis and therefore it is the left hemisphere which is stimulated the most. But football is more than just technical ability! Movement and game sense are a major part of the game. Therefore we must train in such a way that the right hemisphere is also involved. Small games will force it to be involved because the players must make a lot of decisions about movement on and off the ball (time, space, angles).

Although each hemisphere initiates different actions, it is very important that this information is shared to coordinate the final action/output. Transfer of this information takes place through the corpus callosum. For this reason, multi-sensory input and multi-motor output increase the left-right cerebral connections and therefore a wider cortical activity results in more meaningful learning.

This is a form of multi-tasking. Although the initiation for this is in the right hemisphere, it makes sure that all factors involved are meaningful and it stimulates a wider development. Multi-tasking is an extremely important part of brain functioning in football. One must be aware though that multi-tasking on the football pitch is only useful if all the trained tasks serve the same purpose.

To make a quick and good decision, players must be able to access and interpret a huge amount of information. Therefore all factors which are important for the final problem-solving/decision-making need to be assimilated to recognisable patterns.

To stimulate high cognitive thinking it is necessary to involve more variables in your Random Practice that will influence your decision-making (e.g. different shapes, coloured bibs) because those are variable factors that involve the decision-making and determine what you do with the ball in the end. It is not useful to involve tasks that will have no influence on the decision process (e.g. counting numbers, calling unrelated words, ball juggling). Unrelated factors should be kept out when training at this cognitive level.

In conclusion, Random Practice should be introduced at the earliest stage of a player's cognitive and motor skills development. Players at the pre-control skill level and control level should be stimulated to automate their skills as quickly as possible. This will mean a lot of individual work where the player can set his own pace. As long as a motor skill is not settled in an automatic pattern, the player will need his central vision to control the ball. He will have little time for other aspects of the game. Alongside this individual skill work, he needs small-sided random games to make an early connection between all important football elements.

As his skill levels increase, he will progress to the utilisation and proficiency level which allows central vision to be 'freed' for information collection rather than technical chores. At this level, the technical skills are mastered in all kinds of situations and the player will rely more on his peripheral vision to pick up on information about other aspects of the game.

In football, a range of factors will determine whether a player is average, good or excellent (pro level). If we want to create intelligent players, we have to teach them from an early age to make decisions and thereby solve problems in a creative way. Technique, quickness, speed and proprioception are basics that need constant attention outside the formal group training. They need to be automatic so that the player can focus all his attention on planning for the game.

It is in Random Practice that players get a chance to create thought processes that are adaptable and leave room for additional 'memory maps'. It is via Random Practice that the player has the best chance to 'organise' his brain; in other words, the player will optimise his capacity to coordinate existing cognitive structures and combine them into more complex systems.

# Chapter 4

# Teaching Styles
**Richard Cheetham**

In this chapter we will discuss the different teaching styles and which ones are more suitable to stimulate an environment where creativity and decision making are paramount.

I set a group of secondary school children a simple exercise which involved them being asked to draw a watering can. No other instruction (no input in terms of size, shape and colour) was given when the task was set. Just the instruction to draw what had been asked. After a few min they presented their work. Some were 'safe' basic drawings - little imagination but clearly were watering cans. However, a number had added water from the spout going to a plant pot rich in colourful flowers. So why the difference in terms of the end result? Maybe individuality had emerged from the freedom given and lack of too much prescriptive input. It was a wonderful opportunity to see creativity from such a simple task. Therefore the purpose of this section of the book is to encourage greater thought to the adoption of creative teaching and learning, environments that allow that creativity to flourish and a trust in allowing players to try different things, to feel freedom and - as a coach - to be pleasantly surprised at what can emerge. Do we really want a team of players who are products of rigid teaching in the coaching session? Importantly, the purpose of adopting a more creative approach is essential for developing the type of player that is often lacking in football.

This chapter aims to provoke thought through discussion, understanding and comparison of teaching styles. This will allow coaches to decide upon their philosophy and subsequent approach. What are their beliefs in terms of enhancing skill development and do they seek to challenge the players "beyond the replication of techniques and skills", as highlighted by Hastie and Curtner-Smith for research on Teaching Games for Understanding? In effect, we pose the questions "what do I know and how could I be more effective?" Hannaford (1995) states that thought, creativity and learning arise from a range of experiences. Imagine the experiences the players are exposed to in training. Are these broad enough for them to be developed to the greatest potential? It is important that the limitations of the coach do not become the limitations of the player. So let's do our best not to set too many boundaries.

The human being is a 'complex animal' with each having a unique make up and an appreciation of this when coaching will maximise skill development and learning. Are we doing our best to accept and incorporate this individuality? What (and who) allowed the skills of Gascoigne and Bergkamp to emerge? How were these nurtured? Was it because of the style of teaching or in spite of it? So, in among the theory, practices that promote problem solving and integrate meaningful tasks can allow those key skills to develop. The constraints imposed on players often arise from sessions that are limited in scope and imagination and that lack opportunities for individual expression. So often we comment on Spanish and Brazilian players having flair and great skill. These are not genetic attributes but those born out of removing constraints and encouraging a certain amount of freedom. We look at the player, the task, the setting but not always at the coach to see if they have nurtured or inhibited this dynamic. Imagine teaching someone how to play a musical instrument with the best facilities, the best equipment and the most enthusiastic pupil only for the teacher not only to choose the wrong method but never look beyond the most limiting of musical pieces to learn. Football is no different and the increasing percentage of overseas players playing at the highest level in the UK must surely reflect that, somewhere along the line, player development within domestic academies and at grassroots level is failing. That is a bitter pill to swallow!

With knowledge of teaching styles, a 'natural selection' process from the styles available might lead coaches to successfully embrace one in particular to let player attributes fully shine and to foster a highly productive system. The selection of a teaching style depends upon a range of important variables which should be considered. These include the stage of development the players are at, what is trying to be achieved in the session and maybe, more importantly, as stated by Tinning et al (1993), what are the 'beliefs' adopted by the coach in how they approach their work with players and teams?

Of the range of teaching styles which can be applied to learning skills, how many are ever understood or referred to as part of a coach education programme could be questionable. As we all learn in different ways there seems little room for a training session with a "one size fits all" approach to the teaching/delivery of that session. It is said that there are 'a hundred and one ways to skin a cat'. There may be fewer ways to teach a skill but all are worth exploring in order to maximise learning. Also, learning should lead to some form of noticeable and relatively permanent change. So how can an understanding of teaching styles reinforce and maximise this permanence? How can the change be measured and how suitable/appropriate is the approach taken by the coach?

Teaching and learning skills in sport are complex, with a range of variables that need to be recognised and the key is appropriateness and effectiveness. What works in some environments (and with some players) may or may not be transferable, so there needs to be adaptability and flexibility. The teaching styles have been divided into reproduction and production styles. These concepts were developed by Mosston and Ashworth (2002) and, when looked at closely, highlight the issues commented on in Chapter 1. How are creativity and empowerment of players encouraged? Are coaches able to design practice sessions that contain this focus? Each of these will be explored in context and discussed.

## Reproduction styles

Children 'mimic' and copy from a very early age; some of this comes from very deliberate situations such as the development of speech. Copying set patterns of speech can accelerate the child's communication skills. The imitation of those around them in their world is a natural process. This reproduction or 'modelling' is common in coaching, almost a fundamental (but not always the best) starting point when working with junior players. It is one that is often adopted by those new to coaching. The session content is often high on replication of the movement/skill demonstrated and involves repeated practice. The coach tends to adopt a commanding role, setting and controlling the task. There would be few activities here that would replicate a typical game as the practice is so conditioned and the decisions and instruction are coach-led. These do have a place in establishing movement patterns and are not to be diminished in terms of importance but, as we will examine later, they do have limitations and are often over-used. As always, feedback is essential to refine technique and modification of task to achieve the same outcome is vital. As we mentioned earlier, players are all unique and one practice trial may be a more effective and suitable method than others. This is where reproduction styles often lack results because the coach sticks with tried and tested ways or ones that worked for them. However, there is a 'block' when these do not work for all. This 'block' refers to the lack of ability by the coach to present the task differently for those unable to grasp the skill from the teaching style used. Remember the watering can task? Different results were found for the same task, so how hard would it have been to get the group to draw exactly what the coach wanted without some form of variation of presentation of that task? Coaching is no different and this is where the reproduction style is limited. Creativity demanded from players must also go hand in hand with the demand for the creativity of coaches, especially in these situations. The understanding of teaching styles can often lead to better performance from both the player and the coach.

By examining the reproduction style in conjunction with an appreciation of the intellectual capability we all possess, conclusions can be drawn about the merits and pitfalls of this teaching style.

Reflect upon the following during the planning of the coaching session:

- By design these sessions are high in organisation and rigid in structure so there are few opportunities for 'risks' to be taken by the players. The coach has set the boundaries clearly.

- Reproduction styles often contain constant repetition of low level skills such as basic passing, which could be seen as developmentally inappropriate and can be viewed as boring when too much time is spent on these basic skills.

- Activities used in these sessions do not contain the variables found in a game situation and so often lack relevance.

- The "building of skills" should involve an opportunity for the brain and body to be challenged. In other words, do the skill development tasks require the player to use the skills in a decision-making setting?

- Intellectual development should occur alongside the player's physical development so do not exclude 'thinking' exercises and synchronise both. A match is a chaotic place but this 'chaos' is rarely reflected in these coaching environments.

- Reproduction teaching styles do provide a basis for the foundation stone of basic core skills so should be included in the player's learning and development pathway. How often have you heard the phrase "they do the basics well" when referring to a successful team?

If you pass by and take a look at coaching sessions involving children, then note how many times you see them 'lined up' preparing for their chance to demonstrate/practise and how many times you watch unopposed basic tasks. These do not nurture development as effectively as more challenging teaching styles can.

It must be noted that both production and reproduction teaching styles are part of a continuum. In other words, as the players develop, there is a noticeable shift from one style to the other where the move goes from refining/acquiring technique to developing players as competent decision-makers. A coach may use both in the same session. Reproduction style can form part of a warm up or fitness development or reinforce core skills but not dominate the active learning time. Production styles work on situational game/match play and aim to encourage 'responsibility' or 'autonomy' among players, hence a non-reliance on the coach.

## Production styles

Maybe it is in the title, production – being productive! This approach is noticeably different and yet provides its own challenges. With the encouragement of creativity, problem solving and a greater focus on individuality, there are more likely (initially) a greater number of mistakes made and more demands made on both player and coach. The key to understanding and adopting this style involves appreciating what it offers in terms of effectiveness in player development.

The problem solving element (deciding upon a strategy) is a chance for the skills developed and nurtured to be more fully integrated into practice design. Game-related activities can allow the chance to 'throw the reins off' and see how the players respond to given situations - referred to elsewhere in this book as 'free play'. The exercise design is manipulated to focus on the areas worked on and discussed in previous coaching sessions so players have an understanding of the relevance of the preparation and outcome. Very often this may be set around overcoming defensive systems or disrupting attacking team play. There is commonly more than one way and the players decide and take ownership of the problem set. If they have arrived at the strategy and been part of the process, it is more likely they will understand it. If we all used only satellite navigation, then none of us would be able to reach the destination (or end goal) any other way. Production style teaching helps players to map out their routes to goal and remember them!

By being coached this way, players can deal more effectively when in an actual match. A coach issuing instructions ferociously from the sidelines may not have given them the responsibility mentioned earlier or trust to them in training; subsequently they have not taken ownership when it comes to 'live' situations. When we 'learn in context' the brain builds up its resource bank (memories) to cope in competition because situations and likely scenarios will have formed an important part of the coaching programme.

So when does the coach start to use this style in sessions? Is there a 'better' or 'best' time in a player's development and how do they approach it? Children will naturally learn through games and problem solving. They have an incredible capacity at an early age to communicate their needs without words, to adapt to the environment and to challenge themselves (just recall how they manage to achieve those first few steps). Therefore, as has been suggested, synchronise the physical and cognitive development – do not approach them in isolation. Productive teaching styles encourage play and learning in context almost immediately. Ashley Montague refers to play as the "basic ingredient of physical, intellectual, social and emotional growth". The coach needs to appreciate the demands of the task as proportionate to the intellectual and physical development stage of the child when planning the content. This is a challenge and one that coaches should recognise as a part of their vital role and responsibility. It is also important to consider these so expectations are realistic and not set too high. This could lead to disappointment and frustration for both player and coach and, even worse, make the coach more reluctant to try this approach again and 'revert to type'. We always encourage coaches to have confidence and 'faith'.

Our development must be there to optimise the performance and learning of those we coach. Ian McGeechan, the highly regarded coach of Scotland and the British Lions, said: "Never stop learning. Understand that you never know enough ….. the more you listen, the more you see, the better understanding you get, the more you keep moving forward". In terms of reflection, do coaches honestly do this enough?

In terms of production styles, it is important to remember the following in the sessions:

- If the session involves problem solving, challenging the players' intellect, then ensure that small-sided games are included in the process. The smaller the number of players, the more decisions they will make and the more time they will have with the ball.

- Use a more reflective approach and get player feedback; establish why they made the decisions they did.

- The coach develops alongside the players, as they learn to optimise the learning opportunities in the 'deliberate' play scenarios.

- Replication of skill can be gained through passive activities, but in a game, the skill is put in a 'real' context.

The opportunity for children to become more involved with dynamic, demanding and purposeful tasks has a marked effect on motivation and, even more importantly, on retention. We want to keep young players interested and involved at all times and regard that measured 'pressure' as a positive in order to continually think of how these goals can be achieved.

Of great focus is also the emphasis on play. It is within a play environment that they do not simply repeat what is asked but attach meaning through their own exploration. They solved the problem from their efforts and learned from their mistakes – they were not fearful of the consequences from trying!

To conclude, one would hope that the coach can view the options available to them and appreciate the consequences/likely outcomes of both. Throughout this book there is an emphasis on player development, enjoyment and the opportunity to make a significant contribution to the change in approach to football coaching in the UK. The discussion points in this indicate our support for the development and adoption of a production teaching style. This would represent a significant change in the way many coaches work and lead to more engaging and relevant coaching sessions. It is the ability to 'trust' the player, not to suppress the natural inquisitive and exploratory nature of children and to celebrate the moments that show real learning and not just replication and modelling. When remembering this, read the words of Theodore Roosevelt below and see if they are familiar!

"Every child inside him has an aching void for excitement and if we don't fill it with something good which is exciting and interesting and good for him, he will fill it with something which is exciting and interesting and which isn't good for him".

And heed the warning from an advertising campaign by the American Heart Association which once read: **"Caution: children not at play"**!

27

**Chapter 5**

# Philosophy and Methodology for Coaches

The first thing a coach must have is a playing philosophy. We believe this should be a style of play based on passing and maintaining possession, even under pressure. As the game gets quicker, this philosophy will require players who can attack and defend in numbers, improvise, run with the ball, move without the ball, make rapid decisions and quickly perceive what is required in most situations. The coach will need to develop a game pattern and adapt it according to the evolution of the team and the players. To achieve and maintain our philosophy, we believe in the following methods of training:

- Always expose players to realistic game situations. Constantly deny them time and space. Make them play 'in the tight'
- Ensure there is decision-making in every session including the warm up/preparatory phase. Remember, the warm up is a learning environment too, not just a process of preparation
- Emphasise the importance of good communication
- Avoid 'queuing'. Drills destroy skills
- Develop dynamic balance, coordination, agility and speed. Encourage movement off the ball
- Systematic training in the basics of 1 v 1
- Provide players with as many motor experiences as possible, particularly U12s downwards
- Develop an understanding of linkage play and if players cannot go forwards, then go back and start again. Do not allow players to just kick the ball clear. Use free zones where players cannot be tackled
- Teach 'game sense'. Encourage players to solve the problems posed by the game and their opponents, through conditioned games for example
- Allow players to express themselves. Give them free time to be creative and imaginative
- Play with and against older players as this adds to the pressure of time and space
- Allow players to explore different positions as this gives an appreciation of the roles and responsibilities of others
- Look to produce players who are tactically flexible and who can adapt to different systems

## The Parent

Children's sport differs from adult sport in that it is essentially a family activity. Parents are involved at all levels – from emotional and psychological support to practical and financial help. The parent has to drive the player to training sessions and matches, provides the necessary kit and training equipment and pays the match fees and annual subscriptions. The relationship between coach and parent is crucial so the parent must be kept up to date with the philosophy and methodology of the coach at all times. It is vital that the parent is educated along with the player and that the bond between the parent, player and coach is developed and enhanced whenever possible. Unfortunately, parents are often discouraged from involvement and so can develop unrealistic expectations, which benefits no-one, particularly the player. Sadly, parents can make or break their own children.

## The Problem

The belief is that the coaching system in this country has got things wrong, and has done so for many years. There has been an obsession with commitment, work rate and organisation, which has produced structured players, with little flair or confidence on the ball. Where are the great individual players such as Jimmy Greaves, Paul Gascoigne and George Best, who could make things happen for themselves if the game wasn't going their way? The mistake of teaching football as though it was a classroom subject is still evident and many are still doing so. This has failed to take into account that football is an open-skilled game, where the changes are continuous and unpredictable. In a game, players are always reacting to a stimulus, whether it's the ball, an opponent or team-mate. It is therefore essential that the game is the basis for training, since it is artificial to isolate the technical and tactical skills, from the context of the game. It must be remembered that all coordinative actions in football are joined together with the process of decision-making. This is summed up by Professor José Portolés *'There must always be an interaction between the mind and the body'.*

Unfortunately most organised coaching in this country has ignored this and training has involved practising a skill in isolation before putting it into a game. This 'detachment' of the skill from a training situation to the game setting creates preparation without purpose. Why are players doing these if there is no conditioned setting in which to practise them. Training has been dominated by drills, meaning little movement off the ball and no decision-making on the ball. How many times when viewing from the sidelines are there 'queues', where players line up in regimented formation to complete a set skill? Is this specific, is this an effective use of time and, more importantly, is it maximising active learning? This will not improve dribbling skills or teach players how to evade tackles, ride challenges, muscle opponents off the ball, finish clinically or be visually aware. All it has done is diminish the cognitive processes such as attention, decision-making and concentration and bore young players to death and destroy their enthusiasm. In addition, drills only concentrate on a player's central vision, where the visual field is very small and peripheral vision is not required. This is unrealistic because in a game with its numerous variables, peripheral vision information is processed quickly, particularly where motion is concerned, and this allows the visual focus to be directed to other areas of the game. The only positive thing to come out of waiting in line is that it has given players the chance to catch up on conversations with others, perform handstands and cartwheels!

The result is the development of a game style that is unique to this country and based on speed of play and pressure on the ball. Coaches and players have become obsessed with the 'long ball' and have total disregard for possession. Due to a lack of skill, the only thing we can do is play simply. How many times do we hear coaches shout out "play it simple" or "play the way you are facing"? But do players know what this really means and applies to? This has developed into rigid playing roles where we produce right backs or centre forwards who only know that one position, whilst foreign coaching methods produce defenders or mid-field players who can adapt to any roles given to them and who understand the game. Rigid playing styles mean that players are often given jobs due to their inability, not their ability. The desire for a 'destructive midfielder' is a good example, since he is often given the role as he may not be a good passer of the ball, but likes a tackle and the confrontation. The Spanish, however, believe this player should be the most intelligent on the pitch, since if he wins the ball he must have the vision to start an attack or switch play.

From the age of 10, team organisation and positional play seem to be at the very centre of the approach by coaches, when young players are forced into 11 a-side football setting. Watching 10 year olds trying to make sense of the off-side rule and being coached in patterns of play by well-meaning coaches is (both laughable and yet) of great concern. The belief is it should be the development of the individual first and then team organisation, if there is a desire to raise the standards. Instead, our young players are not encouraged to be great individual players and mediocrity emerges. At present there is no philosophy on which to formulate a plan for the future. As coaches, the advantage is that many youngsters between five and ten are healthily obsessed with the game and the first priority must be to maintain that enthusiasm and excitement. Training must therefore be enjoyable and suited to the needs of the players who are being worked with. If not, youngsters will quickly become disillusioned and 'vote with their feet'. How many potential star players have been lost to other sports simply due to poor coaching? Or worse still, lost permanently from sport?

We have already mentioned our philosophy at the start of this introduction, and the methodology that accompanies it. We will now propose a new pathway for the development of youth football, based on small-sided games, where players have to solve the problems of the game for themselves. The benefits of these games are numerous and they can help coaches create a really positive training environment.

Professor José Portolés, currently lecturer of the Spanish Football Federation's Masters degree in football and developer and teacher of the Federation's Football Coaches Licence courses, once pointed out to us that "the player must always be at the centre of the game to learn". These are wise words but from our experience players are often not at the centre of the game because there are too many on the pitch. As a result the game becomes dominated by the biggest, strongest player and so little development takes place. Limiting the numbers in training games, which leads to maximum involvement, would be much more beneficial to learning and to motivation.

From our observations, small-sided games provide enjoyment and learning, as players are getting more touches of the ball and are always involved in the game. At the same time they are practising the fundamental movements of football, such as twisting, turning and making decisions under pressure. They are given more opportunities to attack and defend and have more responsibilities as there are fewer players on the pitch. Most importantly, the playing conditions, such as size and shape of the pitch, number of players and size of the goals, can easily be manipulated by the coach to suit different ages and abilities. We believe this is the best way forward to help the development of young players and provide them with the technical and tactical skills necessary for today's game.

There must be acceptance that the tradition of learning the game in the street (a method still practised in Africa and South America) is largely a thing of the past. Parents may have become too protective, road traffic is higher than at any time and too many alternative options are there. It is no coincidence that our last success in 1966 came with players who learnt the game at street level. Since then, organised coaching has taken over, but with limited success. Only rarely do players such as Gascoigne, Le Tissier and Scholes come through the system and retain their individuality. So what is the way forward? Well, consider the following:

## Create a structured programme:
- Coaches provide their players with game-based training opportunities.
- Programme is age/ability appropriate to those they are working with.
- Programme must be progressive, which incorporates stages of a child's development.
- Coaches know the developmental background of their players so training can progress in a systematic way.

Alongside game-based training, we must also teach fundamental movement skills step by step. Too often, complex sports skills are introduced to young people who have not mastered basic movement patterns. If players have a base of athleticism, specific training will then become more purposeful. Although we are seeing greater and greater athleticism at the elite level of sport, there appears to be less and less at grass roots level and children are leaving primary school without adequate development of their fundamental movement skills. The onus therefore falls on the teacher or coach, not only to teach the skills involved in football but also to ensure that the players practise basic movement training as well.

Physical literacy, which was developed naturally in previous generations, now has to be taught. Previously, children played and competed in several sports so, when they chose to specialise, had a much wider base of transferable motor skills to draw on. Like street football, it is not possible to go back, so one should look at other ways to enhance athleticism. The place to introduce this work is in the warm up and in the book "Warm Ups for Soccer - A Dynamic Approach", it has been shown how time can be used most appropriately to help improve athleticism among our young players. The warm up must therefore become the base for most of our athletic training and this training should continue throughout a player's career.

It is also essential that we put players in athletic situations that cannot be pre-planned and where perception and decision-making become an integral part of the of the movement patterns. This would best represent the variables that they would face in a match situation. We believe this can best be achieved in small-sided games, where players experience many changes of direction and have to anticipate and react to the ball, movement of team mates and opposition. These experiences will occur far more often and with a far greater number of repetitions than in a full 11 a-side game. Therefore a combination of the correct use of the warm up plus training in small-sided games should ensure that the likelihood of producing better football athletes for the future is increased.

Understanding and training athleticism provides a significant challenge to us all and demands a lot of thought and imagination. At present, we believe training is far too conservative, with players rarely being challenged. In my own coaching company, players train on astro-turf, grass slopes, in sand pits, on shale and on any uneven ground we can find, as we believe this is the best way to improve proprioception and force players to deal with any uneven bounce of the ball. The playing environment is safe but challenging. When trying to encourage Academies to do the same, we have only received negative comments. "We cannot put players in situations where they are likely to get injured" is the usual cry. However, we believe the opposite and by always allowing young players to play on perfect pitches, we feel we are failing to challenge their athleticism and so are actually predisposing them to injury.

The idea is not for coaches to passively accept the innovative approach and simply copy a few of the games and training methods and leave things to chance. This would be doing us a disservice, since we see this book merely as a starting point. Whether you agree or not with all or some of what we are saying is not the issue. We want you to approach the book with a completely open mind and be prepared to challenge the concepts and methods that we are proposing, as well as challenge your own philosophy and point of view. Like most aspects of life, the game of football is evolving rapidly, so what is relevant today could be out of date tomorrow. The coach must therefore be prepared to adapt to soccer's ever changing demands, so we need creative, innovative and forward thinkers working with children. Those who simply repeat what they did as players will fail to recognise or understand the developmental stages that young players pass through and therefore cease to lay the foundations for future learning. The future we refer to needs to be in safe hands. We need to question why so many foreign players appear more talented than English players and yet the Football Association and clubs are investing millions of pounds in youth football. Perhaps it is something to do with the structure and methods used. As Einstein once said: *"Learn from yesterday, live for today, hope for tomorrow. The important thing is to not stop questioning."*

**Chapter 6**

# Attachment and Detachment

**Attachment**
Connection with – combination with – linkage with

**Detachment**
Disconnection from – separation from

As we will show in chapter 7, there must be vertical attachment, assimilation or linkage between each double age group in order to maximise a player's development. Without this attachment material is often repeated, which can be boring and put players off training, or progressions are missed out completely, which has a negative effect on learning. However, there must also be attachment within each training session so that players see a connection between the warm-up, group section and team section. Unfortunately, from our observation, this rarely happens and we regularly watch sessions in which there is no theme running through them or any connection between the various practices. In the next chapter, coaches will be shown how to link double age groups vertically from 5 to 16 years of age, but first need to understand how to provide horizontal attachment in each training session in order to make optimum use of their time with the players.

To provide horizontal attachment, each training session should follow a format since, in order to get something done, the brain follows a certain neurological pattern, changing information into actions. The information is gathered as follows: arousal, orientation and execution, so it is vital to run a training session along similar lines so that players understand the objective that is trying to be achieved.

## Warm up (Arousal)
Coaches must start with an activity that gets players up for playing, as it is critical to arouse the mind and body. So there must be no static stretching or slow jogs around the field! As well as dynamic flexibility, the arousal should include competition, decision-making, reaction to a stimulus and an awareness of time and space. Arousal games could include handball, touch rugby, tag, basketball and floor hockey. All movement training must be carried out as part of the arousal, including acceleration, deceleration, agility, speed, coordination, dynamic balance and functional strength, when the players are fresh. The movement patterns must be related to the game and carried out with intensity and precision. Above all, this part of the session must be appealing and fun.

## Group Practice (Orientation)

Once players have been aroused, switch to group activity practices such as 1 v 1, 2 v 2, 3 v 3 and 4 v 4 games, as well as numbers up and numbers down situations. The games should be appropriate for the age group and should relate to the objective for the session. Group practice should make up the bulk of training in order to maximise ball contacts, decision-making and game awareness. Coaching must be limited and players should be guided towards their objectives, not given constant instructions. The main emphasis should be on individual tactics and basic group tactics, which are defined as 'dynamic repetition' since the same or similar situations will keep on occurring. This should teach the players the fundamentals of attack and defence and allow them to work on simple tactics in every imaginable situation. This part of the session is crucial because, unless players develop an understanding of basic small group attacking and defending patterns, they will be ill-prepared to work within a large team teaching practice, as outlined below.

## Team Practice (Execution)

Finally the coach should switch to a game which puts the group practice into a realistic game situation. This could be linkage play or attacking a line or goal, and should encourage players to make tactical decisions and find tactical solutions to problems in the larger game. The coach needs to create a picture for players and offer tips during the game without stopping it, but most of the time should allow them to play and solve their own problems. Certainly the key to developing game sense lies in giving young players the chance to play in realistic games, whilst gradually increasing the complexity of the task.

Arousal and group practice must take priority over team practice until a player reaches his early teens. Only then should the coach dedicate equal time to game activity practice as team play and position-specific play start to take shape. However, players between 12 and 14 should start to familiarize themselves with different positional roles before they start to specialise. True specialisation should begin at about 15 years of age, when coaches can begin to see which roles players are suited to, but even then players should always be free to switch positions.

The type of game chosen by the coach will have a major impact on the number of ball receptions and decision-making opportunities each player is exposed to. The coach therefore has to plan each session carefully in order to maximise technical repetition (dynamic repetition), movement and decision-making and decide the percentage of time dedicated to each game form. To work alongside the vertical method of attachment, we would suggest the following horizontal method of attachment for each double age group, in order to maximise learning.

## 5/6 years of age – session one hour

The traditional division of football training into warm-up, group activity and team activity is not appropriate for this age group. They do not need to start each session with a structured warm-up, but with unstructured play in order to let off steam. The rest of the session should be divided between little games and various physical activities. The former will involve lots of individual work with the ball, which must focus on dribbling in traffic, requiring visual awareness along with unstructured small-sided games. The physical aspect gives the coach a chance to introduce the five basic ways of moving (walking and crawling, running, hopping and jumping, skipping and galloping) as well as an understanding of the four areas of space. However, they must be introduced in a fun way and built on the strength of a young child's vivid imagination.

Each training session should last no longer than an hour and no single activity should last longer than 15 min, as children at this age quickly lose concentration. The most important thing for them is to have fun since their first introduction to training often decides their eventual level of interest in the game. Providing a programme filled with lots of positive experiences might ensure a child's long-term interest in the game.

## 7/8 years of age – session one hour

### Warm-up (20 min)
- As this is the first window of opportunity for coordination, the coach should include lots of different ways of moving (skipping, hopping, galloping, jumping etc) and combine them in a series of movements.
- It is also the first window of opportunity for speed and should be introduced in the form of relays and tag games.
- Arousal games could include basketball, handball and floor hockey, which involve throwing, catching, rolling, dribbling, striking, and bouncing.

### Group Practice (25 min)
1 v 1, 2 v 1, 2 v 2, 3 v 1, 3 v 2 and 3 v 3

### Team Practice (15 min)
4 v 4

## 9/10 years of age – session one hour 30 min

### Warm-up (30 min)
- Reinforce previous work including combination movements, tag games, relays and multi-sports.
- Precision training involving acceleration, deceleration, agility and quick feet must now be taught.
- Introduce functional strength work and low level plyometrics.

### Group Practice (40 min)
- 1 v 1, 2 v 1, 2 v 2, 3 v 1, 3 v 2, 3 v 3 and 4 v 4
- Provide lots of little games and competitions which are playful and easy to understand.

### Team Practice (20 min)
- Play 5 v 5
- Show the start of linkage play and introduce goalkeepers.

## 11/12 years of age – session one hour 30 min

### Warm-up (30 min)
- Reinforce previous work including dynamic flexibility, tag games, relays and multi-sports.
- Combine speed, dynamic balance and agility movements as part of the coordination programme.
- Introduce the three planes of movement and start by working a player on his own, then mirroring a partner and finally mirroring a partner with a ball.
- Progress to simple chaos training.
- Continue with movement-based strength training, using low level plyometrics, own body weight and a partner.

### Group Practice (35 min)
- 1 v 1, 2 v 1, 2 v 2, 3 v 1, 3 v 2, 3 v 3 and 4 v 4
- Teach the fundamentals of 1 v 1 attacking and simple group tactics in 2 v 1 situations.
- Train players to defend in pairs and learn to cover and drop off.

### Team Practice (25 min)
- Play 6 v 6 and 7 v 7 with goalkeepers.
- Continue linkage play and emphasise building from the back and playing through mid-field.

## 13/14 years of age – session one hour 30 min

### Warm-up (30 min)
- Reinforce previous work including tag games, relays, multi-sports, acceleration, deceleration, coordination and dynamic balance.
- Continue movement-based strength work with a partner, own body weight and medicine balls.
- Continue with intermediate level plyometrics if players are capable of participating.
- Develop soccer-specific chaos training with players working in groups of three or four.
- Work on the first step and in all three planes of movement.
- Do not introduce new material.

### Group Practice (30 min)
- 1 v 1, 2 v 1, 1 v 2, 2 v 2, 3 v 3, 2 v 3, 4 v 4 and 3 v 4
- Enhance coordination with lots of 1 v 1 and 1 v 2 situations.

### Team Practice (30 min)
- Play 6 v 6, 7 v 7, 8 v 8 and 9 v 9, as well as numbers up and numbers down.
- Develop linkage play in a 1 - 3 - 3 - 2 formation.
- Play from penalty area to penalty area and width of penalty area.
- This is the first stage of intensive tactics training.

## 15/16 years of age – session one hour 30 min

### Warm-up (25 min)
- Change of direction, change of speed and change of rhythm activities, in order to re-learn how to control the body.
- Reinforce all previous work but add position-specific chaos training. Continue with multi-sports.
- Systematic strength training programme using own body weight, a partner, medicine balls, viprs and circuit training.
- Continue to work on intermediate level plyometrics but be aware of the risks.
- Promote speed exercises in constantly changing situations and combine them with the techniques of football.

### Group Practice (30 min)
- Play 1 v 1, 2 v 2, 3 v 3 and 4 v 4
- Make the games more physically and mentally demanding e.g. man-to-man marking.

**Team Practice (35 min)**

- Play 6 v 6, 7 v 7, 8 v 8, 9 v 9 and 11 v 11
- Continue with linkage play and start with a 1 – 4 – 4 – 2 formation.
- Develop patterns of play and position-specific training. Learn tactics without an opponent, with a passive opponent and then with an active opponent.
- This latter stage must not be missed out as players have to be aware of the movement and intentions of their opponents.
- Players should be encouraged to plan tactical actions, carry them out and then evaluate them.

If players are to reach their full potential, then it is important to follow a systematic approach to training. This is because the brain is designed to perceive and generate patterns and when players identify and connect new and previous material, their brain links the new information with the old, which develops long term memory. If they connect the new with the old and gain more experience, they will create new patterns, which they can fall back on when confronted with new situations. It is essential to develop physical intelligence (technique, movement and athleticism) with tactical intelligence (the ability to see space, shapes and patterns), so that in a game the player can control the ball instantly and at the same time evaluate his options.

Too often players lack both physical and tactical intelligence, due to incorrect training, and this limits the level of football they will play. Physical and tactical intelligence must be developed in an attached, not detached, way if we want to maximise a player's ability. For example, in order to develop tactical intelligence it is essential to start with individual tactics, progress to small group tactics and finish with team tactics, when players are able to fully understand the concepts involved. Unfortunately, young players are often presented with team tactics and structure before they are ready and so fail to develop their tactical intelligence sufficiently, which will prevent them competing at the highest level.

**Chapter 7**

# The Structure of Youth Football

We believe the first thing that must change is the present structure of youth football. Traditionally, we classify players according to chronological age and this applies to most youth sports around the world. However, many aspects of soccer performance at this age are related to biological maturity. As a result, a normal or late developing child who plays against an early maturer may be at a huge disadvantage trying to compete with a stronger, faster opponent. Identifying an early or late developer must be an important factor when determining long term development plans.

## The problem with the present system

- Everything is based on a child's chronological age not biological age
- We do not plan what to coach and at what time in the development of young football players
- Limited emphasis on creating an enjoyable training environment
- Too much time is spent on drills, which are ineffective and time-consuming
- Lack of understanding of the demands (both physical and mental) in practices and competition in relation to the capacities of the children
- There is no systematic programme in place to develop young footballers
- Very little training is provided to help develop children's body management skills such as core skills and injury treatment and prevention
- Children are forced to adapt to the competition and its rules instead of the other way round
- We make the traditional mistake of compartmentalising the coaching of soccer into certain disciplines (technique, tactics and physical fitness)
- Children are usually taught the game in parts which are not integrated into a dynamic whole situation
- Too many skills taught in isolation and detached from others
- Young players are rarely given time to be creative and expressive
- We give players set positions and force them to play in a set way from a young age
- Players are fearful of making mistakes thus creating an unhealthy learning environment
- Maximising player involvement is not focussed on enough, with too many full sized games in practice
- There are very few coaches who understand child development.

To help overcome many of these problems, we suggest there should be six levels of progressive development based on double age groups. By running two or more teams at each double age group, it would be possible to move players up and down according to ability and physical maturity. We see this as a more meaningful way of separating players into their appropriate training groups. In turn, it should be easier for coaches to confront players with problems and coaching situations that are not beyond their capabilities. However, for this to happen, the coach must understand the step by step approach to learning, where roughly every two years the difficulty and complexity of training should increase in harmony with the physical and intellectual growth of their players. Unfortunately, too often children are put into game situations which are beyond their scope at that particular stage of their development and this can cause great frustration. It is therefore essential that the coach understands how children learn and recognises when to progress to the next stage of their development.

The Importance of Age Appropriate Training for Young Players
It is essential that young footballers are allowed to progress slowly from one unit or game to the next, with slightly more difficult and complex situations to solve. This is no different to how we teach literacy or numeracy in school. There is no progression until the technical and tactical requirements of one game have been understood and mastered. We are confident this football development model will give young players 11 years of effective and enjoyable practice, which will result in them becoming more intelligent, more creative and more complete footballers.

## Lines of Interaction

All coaches must understand why there has to be a systematic development programme for children. They must also understand the lines of interaction, which are the maximum number of possible passing options between players in a game. As more players enter the field of play, more lines of interaction become possible and the more challenging and complex the tactical situations become. This immediately has a direct impact on the players' decision-making, as it becomes much harder to see the game.

The following diagrams illustrate this more clearly:

## 2 lines of interaction

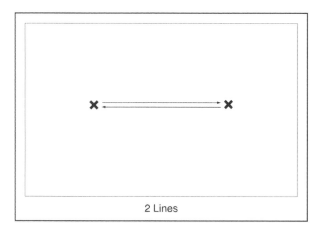

2 Lines

## 6 lines of interaction

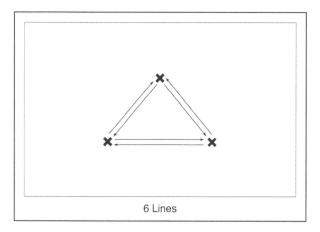

6 Lines

## 12 lines of interaction

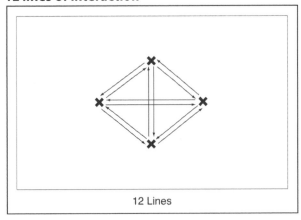

12 Lines

The table below gives a clear indication of the number of possible lines of interaction between players, according to the size of the game and why this can become a tactically overwhelming problem for many children.

3 v 3    =   30 lines of interaction
4 v 4    =   56 lines of interaction
5 v 5    =   90 lines of interaction
6 v 6    = 132 lines of interaction
7 v 7    = 182 lines of interaction
8 v 8    = 240 lines of interaction
9 v 9    = 306 lines of interaction
10 v 10 = 310 lines of interaction
11 v 11 = 462 lines of interaction

More lines of interaction make for a tactically more complex situation. For 7 year olds, playing in a 7 v 7 game, there are 152 more potential lines of interaction than in a 3 v 3 game. As a result, the tactical problems become far too complicated to solve, as the players cannot make sense of the incoming information, as they don't have the memory capacity. Players then fail to see the smaller team shapes (triangles, diamonds, lines and squares) on which the basic understanding of tactics is based. If players don't see these small team shapes or have an understanding of distance, angles and time, then they are unlikely to be in the correct position and so won't be able to perform their role in the team. Basic tactics are about correct positioning and since distances and angles are constantly changing, players have to continually re-evaluate their position in the ever-changing environment. In a 3 v 3 game it is easier for 7 year olds to do this, as they are always involved in the game. Also, a 7 year old has not developed the peripheral vision to cope with more than this.

Similarly, for 13 and 14 year olds there are 222 more potential lines of interaction in an 11 v 11 game than in an 8 v 8 game. Many foreign associations recognise that 8 v 8 and 9 v 9 are a better option than 11 v 11 at this age, since many of the group tactics involve 2, 3 or 4 players around the ball and is a tactical situation which most 13 year olds can understand. Research by Grant et al (1999) compared 8 v 8 with 11 v 11 and discovered the following:

- In 8 v 8 players covered a greater distance and spent less time standing still

- They completed more activities when in possession of the ball

- They attempted more short distance passing and less long distance passing than in 11 v 11

- Technical demands were higher as players were involved in more activities with the ball e.g. passing and changing direction

We must make sure that young players are only put in game situations where they have the experience and cognitive maturity to carry out team tactics. Instead we introduce complicated team tactics before players have the necessary perceptual skills needed to cope. Is it any wonder that many of our young players fail?

We believe our football development model can be compared favourably with children learning to read. Young children start by first recognising letters, then parts of words, then complete words and finally sentences. Once they have reached this degree of competence, it provides them with the confidence, stimulation and skills needed to enjoy reading books of ever increasing complexity. This step by step approach to reading is represented by the books below and the order in which they are likely to be read. The comparable stages of football development have been placed underneath.

**Postman Pat**      **Charlie and the Chocolate Factory**  **The Famous Five**
1v1                3v3                      4v4/5v5

**Harry Potter**      **Lord of the Rings**      **Macbeth**
6v6/7v7              8v8/9v9              11v11

Just as with academic education, a young player's football education must be progressive. However, for some reason, when it comes to football, children are often placed in complex situations before they are able to handle basic fundamental motor skills or understand size, shape and space. To make it worse, those between 5 and 12 years old are routinely put into formal positions at an age when their technical ability and spatial awareness are not sufficiently developed to enable them to have an understanding of large team tactics. In school we do not expect them to be able to tackle Shakespeare's Macbeth before they have mastered The Famous Five, but in football, we often miss out Postman Pat (1v1) completely, start with The Famous Five (5v5), progress to Harry Potter (7v7) and move straight to Shakespeare (11v11). In fact, in many cases, we even miss out The Famous Five and start with Harry Potter! As a result, there is little player development, as they are often overwhelmed by the amount of information they have to process. We end up with the 'kick and rush' game we see every week in the park.

## Suggested six stages of development:

### Module One (5 and 6 year olds)
Training and playing should be fun and a priority here. At this age children have limited concentration spans and are easily distracted so it is important not to spend time on repetitive practices. It is essential that this age group develops a variety of fundamental skills to help them become good athletes, before they start training in a specific sport. Any competition at this stage must be small-sided and informal. Players need to use a variety of balls and should practise throwing, catching, bouncing, rolling and dribbling, as well as kicking - they should be allowed to treat the ball as a toy. At the same time the coach must make each child aware of the different aspects of space (self space, closed space, open space and general space) and then challenge them to think about spatial considerations in their games.

At this level the training activities should only be seen as another fun activity that just happens to include a football. Children at this age are not ready for football-specific information and there should be no emphasis on team concepts or positional play. The information the players receive from the coach should only be about each individual's relationship with the ball. Therefore, each player must always want the ball, feel comfortable with the ball and keep the ball close to them. As Alan Ball always said "Children need to master the ball or the ball will master them". This crucial stage of development is one that cannot be approached incorrectly if we want to produce creative and exciting players for the future!

The five basic ways of moving - walking/crawling, running, hopping, skipping and galloping - must also be a major part of the developmental process at this level. However, good balance must be acquired before a child can become competent at hopping, skipping and galloping, so the coach must work on activities with this age group which stimulate and enhance this key component. Certainly, we see balance as the foundation to all athletic movement, so the more balance becomes a part of a child's athletic development, the better he or she will become at performing more complicated tasks, whether they be motor skills or specific sport skills.

If we want skilful children, then we must ensure that they quickly develop advanced coordination patterns in their locomotive skills, which will eventually help them to reach their full potential. Unfortunately, coordinated movement patterns are often not in place by six years of age, either through poor physical education programmes, lack of knowledge among coaches or a lack of practice. To make it worse, children are often trained in situations where little or no spatial awareness is required. Since all movement occurs in space, those children who have a better understanding of it are able to move more safely. The concept of spatial awareness should therefore be taught from the start of the programme.

Physical literacy, gained through a child's early movement experiences, underpins all aspects of an individual's subsequent development in sport and physical activity. It is essential that, at Module One, young players get a variety of agility skills, both in the air and on the ground, before they start training in a specific sport. Apart from mastering the five ways of moving, they must also be able to roll, tumble, balance, bounce, jump with a twist and turn etc, as developing these gymnastic skills provides a solid foundation for athletic development that leads towards sports specialisation at a later age.

Studies by Nagormi (1977), Harre (1982) and Baker, Cote and Abernethy (2003) all recommend a multi-lateral approach to training before the age of 12, in order to produce better athletes and expert decision-makers. From their research, early specialisation led to quick performance improvements, but this was rarely maintained and many players were burnt out by 18 years of age, with many giving up. Although there was slower improvement at the start using multi-lateral programmes, transfer of learning occurred earlier rather than later in the athlete's development. The implication that can be drawn from these studies is that early specialisation may not be necessary in decision-making sports like soccer.

Unfortunately, children are frequently taught games before they are able to adequately perform fundamental motor skills. This situation is made worse by mounting evidence which suggests that very few children are sufficiently active enough to develop these skills. To avoid failure and embarrassment we feel it is necessary at this age to focus on the development of essential motor skills alongside a multi-lateral programme.

## Module Two (7 and 8 year olds)

Football training at this level should still be a fun activity where players are encouraged to experiment with the ball. Building comfort with the ball will provide players with a variety of crucial skills which they will need as they get older. Coaches should therefore always start each session by reinforcing the work introduced at level one, so the emphasis will be on 1 v 1, 2 v 1 and 2 v 2. They should then progress to a programme of simplified games of 3 v 3 and 4 v 4. 3 v 3 is the optimum game at this level, as it is the perfect introduction to learning triangular support shapes in terms of angles and distances, both in defence and attack. As angles and distances are constantly changing, players have to continually re-evaluate their position in ever-fluctuating situations. However, young players at this age will not understand terms such as angles or shapes, so the coach has to simplify things by asking questions such as "can the ball get to you?" or "can you get the ball to your player?" There should be no fixed positions - this will avoid early specialisation - and continuous repetition in simplified games will help develop game sense and judgement. With many more ball contacts, the technical skills of dribbling, passing, receiving and tackling will be acquired more easily.

The more opportunities each player has with the ball, in fun games, the better that player will be. As we keep emphasising, the child must be at the centre of the game in order to learn. It's therefore important that we do not train in games high in numbers at this age. If we do, the physically more mature players stand out due to their extra strength and speed, whilst the rest are left on the periphery of the game, unable to get involved. The larger games also cause a tactical problem, in that players have to be in two different positions depending on who has the ball. When playing 7 v 7, the ball changes sides continuously, so players get stuck in a 'no man's land' of changing possession, as they cannot move or think faster than the ball. No sooner do they start moving in one direction than they have to move back in the opposite direction. However, by playing 3 v 3, it is easier to concentrate on the need to keep possession, so players learn to deal with the moments of transition that continually occur in the game.

## Attacking in 3 v 3

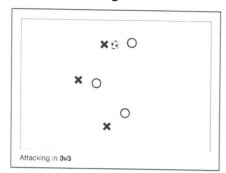

Attacking in **3v3**

## Defending in 3 v 3

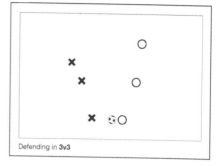

Defending in **3v3**

Ideal for attacking
Xs can:
Go forwards, backwards,
left or right

Ideal for defending
Xs have:
Pressure
Cover
Balance

- 3 v 3 is a valuable starting point as it is the game that involves the smallest shape, the triangle.
- The extra space encourages players to spread out.
- 3 v 3 teaches the basic shape of the game and players naturally form triangles with no mention of tactics.
- 3 v 3 enables young players to play on the field and find their position in space according to their role, the ball, team mates and opposition. With so few players, everybody must take responsibility.
- 3 v 3 enables young players to begin dealing with the four moments of play - losing the ball and regaining possession or being in possession and then losing the ball. They start to learn that they must be in two different positions depending on who has the ball.
- This approach encourages the less assertive to become involved and offers them the opportunity to grow in confidence.
- Athletic growth is enhanced due to the continual movement of the players.

At Module Two, players should be more advanced in their locomotive skills and so need to start combining movements since football is not always about one movement but several, often at the same time. These could include the same movements but in different directions e.g. skipping forwards, backwards and sideways but in any order or combination of three different movements, such as skipping forwards, galloping backwards and shuffling sideways. Using dynamic flexibility exercises as part of the warm up is also a great way of improving locomotive co-ordination and control at this age. Simple tag games should also be introduced at this level in order to improve random agility and force players to process perceptual information more quickly.

It is also at this age that we get the first window of opportunity for improving speed. Sprinting practices (up to 20 metres) should be part of training and involve changes of direction and speed variation eg jog-sprint-jog-sprint. First, however, children must be shown simple exercises for improving coordination and sprinting technique. In addition, own body weight should be used for strength work and include jumping, combination jumping (hop-hop-jump or hop-step-jump) and skipping. This should be the start of a progressive plyometric programme.

### Module Three (9 and 10 year olds)
Coaches start by reinforcing the work introduced at Module One and Two and then progress to games of 4 v 4 (without goalkeepers) and 5 v 5 (with goalkeepers). These simplified games teach the basic diamond shape, which ensures good angles and distances of support wherever the ball might be and gives the player an understanding of width, length and depth. This shape enables players to play forwards, backwards or sideways, in a game-like situation, which children of this age can easily recognise. 4 v 4 provides the minimum numbers needed for all the principles of play as listed below.

| | |
|---|---|
| Tail of the diamond (nearest to goal): | Central defender (supplies depth) |
| Right side of the diamond: | Right mid-fielder (supplies width) |
| Left side of the diamond: | Left mid-fielder (supplies width) |
| Head of the diamond: | Central attacker (supplies penetration) |

### Ideal attacking shape

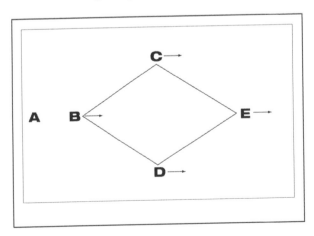

- C and D give the team attacking width
- E gives the team attacking length
- B gives the team balance and support in mid-field
- If goalkeeper A is added, he acts as support as the ball can be passed back to him. This will encourage players to 'start again' if they cannot go forwards

**Ideal defending shape**
- Players C and D tuck in centrally, as the middle is the dangerous part of the field
- Player E drops back into mid-field to track defenders who have gone forward
- Player B drops off to provide depth
- If goalkeeper A is added, he drops back into position and is responsible for the space in front of him and behind B

In the games players should be encouraged to take up a flexible diamond shape at set pieces such as goal kicks and for the throw in. When the ball is in play, all players should look to contribute when attacking and help to defend when possession is lost. It is important that players rotate positions so that they experience all roles in the shape. This should improve their perception as they will be forced to see things from different angles as well as appreciate the demands of those other positions.

Every warm up should continually revisit the movement foundation work of the previous levels, before progressing athletic training to the next stage. At Module Three, speed training becomes essential as we need to teach the nervous system how to fire the muscles quickly and train the central nervous system. Although the players do not have the muscle mass required for speed, they do have an almost fully developed nervous system. Neural activation and fast twitch muscle fibre recruitment can contribute a great deal to future speed capacities.

Acceleration is often the key to soccer performance and is the most trainable component of speed. Acceleration at this age should be trained in the context of posture, arm action and leg action and only when the correct mechanics have been taught and mastered should we make the drills competitive. Competition can best be achieved in simple 1 v 1 races, where one player has to react to the movements of the other. Things can then be taken a stage further by adding different patterns and changes of direction to the races.

Equally critical to soccer performance is the ability to decelerate as quickly as possible, in order to make another movement. Deceleration is not just stopping under control but changing direction whilst trying to maintain momentum and is an essential part of soccer. Stopping involves bending at the hip, knee and ankle, in order to reduce force, allowing the muscles that cross these joints to act as shock absorbers. Again, the correct mechanics must be taught since it is during deceleration that most injuries and performance errors occur.

Once acceleration and deceleration have been taught, it now becomes essential to speed up the transition between them. We can achieve this by playing tag games, which will promote directional changes, reaction speed and changes of pace. We must then bridge the gap between athletic training and speed training by using a ball. Improving a player's technical competence and speed of execution of movements with a ball will help develop game speed. This integrated approach to movement with and without the ball becomes increasingly important at this stage of speed development.

## Module Four (11 and 12 year olds)

Coaches start by reinforcing the work of the previous three levels and then progress to games of 6 v 6 (without goalkeepers) and 7 v 7 (with goalkeepers). The reasons for this are as follows:

- It is an easier transition from 5 v 5 than going straight to 9 v 9 or 11 v 11
- Players continue to develop technically under match conditions and learn how to use this technique in simple tactical situations
- It is far easier to understand than 11 v 11
- With fewer players on the pitch, they have far more ball contacts than in 11 v 11 and players are always in the game through anticipatory movements as well as actual ball work
- Players attack and defend the penalty area more often and the shorter distances provide players with more experience of goal kicks, free kicks, corners and throw ins
- They can use the whole field and change the point of attack, unlike 11 a-side
- The pitch is small enough to allow all players to interact within a game situation
- Players are routinely put into formal positions at this age when their spatial awareness and technical range do not lend themselves to an understanding of larger group tactics
- The introduction of zones enables players start to understand transition and linkage play
- Games do not depend on strength and power, but technical ability and game sense

## Pyramid shape

The pyramid shape will guarantee that children at this age understand width and depth and this is a natural progression towards the large game. They must start to see that team shapes are made up of smaller inter-connecting shapes, mainly triangles, diamonds, squares and lines, and it is the ability to see and understand these smaller shapes that can eventually decide whether a player is a success or failure.

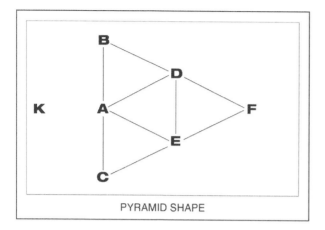

PYRAMID SHAPE

Once players have understood the basic pyramid shape, introduce transition games of 6 v 6 and 7 v 7 with goalkeepers, where players maintain shape and balance by using zones.

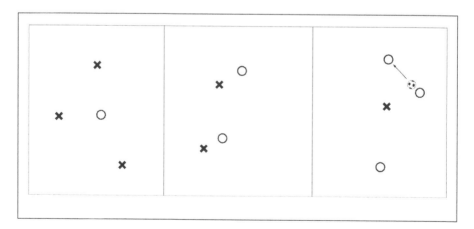

- Start off with a 3 v 1 overload in each defensive third, so that players have a chance to build up from the back
- At the start players stay in their own zones, so they get an understanding of team shape
- Once players get an understanding of link play, allow them to move zones.

- However, once possession is lost, they immediately drop back into their own third, to allow the other team a chance to develop play

At Module Four lateral speed and agility training now becomes an essential part of the movement programme. Agility, which is the ability to stop effectively under control and change direction, is essential for football and should be in place by 11 years of age. Agility can be planned or reactive. Planned agility occurs when a player knows when and where they are going to move before they begin a change of direction. However, in football nearly all the situations are reactive and cannot be pre-planned. Instead, players have to rely on information such as ball flight and the movement of team mates and opponents before they respond. Why then do we place cones on the ground to define an agility pattern, as players can now pre-plan their movements? Cones should only be used to teach basic body positioning and once players understand this, then the cones must be removed.

To be seen as agile, a player must be able to coordinate the deceleration and acceleration phases simultaneously. This is known as transition and depends on how quickly a player can assess the situation and reposition his body, which will set him up for a smooth, efficient transition from one movement or direction to another.

*'Agility is a change of speed or change of direction in response to a stimulus'*
(Australian Institute of Sport)

Agility has four key components:

1. Control of body position
2. Quick feet
3. Strength and power
4. Reaction to environment

## Control of body position
When running forward, planting, turning to the left and running back the way you came (a complete 180o turn), the majority of the breaking forces should be on the left leg (inside leg). When done correctly, if the player is turning to his left, he should start the breaking process with his right leg. He should then make half the turn (90o) by the time the left heel hits the ground. This will fire the left hamstrings and calves, as the player starts to sit into the cut and lean the upper body in the direction he wants to go. This position should look like a lateral lunge, with the upper body leaning

over the inside leg. By the time the right foot hits the ground again (outside leg), most of the force has been reduced and the right leg can start the acceleration phase.

Too many players use the outside leg (right leg in this example) as the primary decelerator, which causes the body mass to shift towards the outside leg and away from the direction the player wants to go. This merely slows the transition from deceleration to acceleration and puts great strain on the knee joints.

We must start by teaching the basic body position, so set out the cones in a W shape, about five metres apart. The players cut around each cone at half speed, concentrating on body position and good feet and then progress by going into the cut at half pace and coming out at full speed. Once players have understood the movements, remove the cones and let them move randomly in the grid. This will make them react to the other players and force them to make adjustments in angles, speed and deceleration mechanics. Finish with a group activity such as a tag game or an appropriate small-sided game.

## Quickness

The second component of agility is quickness and is essential to the other three components. Quickness is all movement within one metre of the body and could be forward, back, sideways, up or down, and usually involves one to four steps. The main aim of quick feet is to decrease ground contact time and increase the rate of force production. We can only speed up, slow down, and turn when one foot is in contact with the ground, so the faster we can move our feet off the ground and back down, the quicker we will be.

The practical must start with quick feet chops, where the toes are raised two or three centimetres and the feet touch the ground as many times as possible in 10 seconds. Players count their own touches and then try to beat that score. Once players have understood the movement, they do the same thing but shift their feet from side to side and forward and back. Then progress to a game where they are competing against another player and finish with a tag game or an appropriate small-sided game.

## Strength and Power

The muscular system is organised in such a way that when we play football we use groups of muscles, not a single muscle. Movements consist of multiple joint, multiple muscle activities so it is essential that we train movements and not muscles! Training joints in isolation is counter-productive to efficient movement as it can create confusion in the neural pathways.

There is some evidence to suggest that the training of youth players at this level does not need to focus on improving physical performance. We would disagree with this statement, although if we are working on strength and power, we must be aware that there is a large difference in individual maturation within this age group. Therefore players of a similar skeletal age should always be paired up. When working on this component of agility, we must always use functional activities out on the field, which will help improve technical and tactical skills at the same time.

Football is one of the most difficult games to play because most football skills are performed on one leg. Single-leg strength is a quality that is often ignored in training sessions but is essential to the improvement of speed and balance and the prevention of injury. It is therefore vital that single-leg strength becomes the focal point of a functional strength and power programme. Many of the practical exercises will be single-leg, with the player using his own body weight for resistance. The following game would be a good example of this:

Players move and pass several balls by hand. When not in possession, players hop anywhere in the grid. However, as soon as they receive a pass, they put in a short sprint, pass to a player who is hopping and then return to hopping themselves. Finish with a tag game or an appropriate small-sided game.

## Reaction Speed

Reaction speed is the ability to react quickly to unforeseen actions of the ball, opponents or team mates. Reaction speed is very much dependent on the visual stimuli that the player processes to make decisions. Perceiving the situation, anticipating what might happen and then deciding what to do all have an influence on reaction speed. Although performing a drill repeatedly can produce accurate movements, during a game a player encounters nothing as predictable as a drill.

If a player wishes to be successful in the game, he has to minimise reaction time. Three basic parameters influence reaction **Time:** the environment that causes the thought for action, the time between the thought for action and the initiation of the action and the time between the initiation of the action and its completion. The player with a slower reaction time will have fewer opportunities to be successful. It is also useful to refer to 'anticipation' in sessions. Here players are made aware of the need to be alert and ready and demonstrate this in their stance and preparation. Football is such a fast-moving game that they need to always be ready to react and to anticipate, which further reduces reaction time.

The most valuable method of developing reactive agility is through the use of small-sided or conditioned games. Such games allow young players to experience all the change of direction situations and perceptual information sources that occur in the real game but the coach can ensure a greater number of practice opportunities or repetitions compared to a real game. The games can also be overloaded to create situations that are more difficult than a normal game.

The practical should start with players working in pairs with the following activity creating a setting to challenge and enhance reactive agility:

A and B face each other on opposite sides of an imaginary line, five metres in length, with A the attacker and B the defender. A uses a sudden change of speed and direction to move laterally up and down the line. B attempts to react to his moves as quickly as possible. Players change roles every 20 seconds. Next A moves forwards and backwards whilst facing B. B has react to A's moves as quickly as possible. Finally, combine both movements. A works from side to side or forwards and backwards and B has to react to the movements. Change roles every 20 seconds. This is an example of a reaction game and the action should be completed with a tag game or appropriate small-sided game.

## Dynamic Balance
Dynamic balance underpins all our speed and agility work and occurs every time we transfer our weight. Therefore we have to regain balance and maintain balance every time we walk, jog, run, start, stop, skip, hop, jump and gallop. When children can master these movements, it becomes much easier to kick, throw, catch, dribble, volley, strike with a bat, strike with a racquet, strike with a stick and so on. The reason that football is such a difficult game to play is because it is unipodolic. This simply means that most of the game is spent standing on one leg so every time a player walks, jogs, runs, kicks a ball, passes a ball, volleys a ball, dribbles a ball and shoots, he is standing on one leg. In fact, the only time a player stands on two legs in football is when he is standing still. To play football well, players have to master dynamic balance and be proficient at it by the end of level four.

## Module Five (13 and 14 year olds)
Coaches should start by reinforcing the work of the previous four levels and then progress to games of 8 v 8 (without goalkeepers) and 9 v 9 (with goalkeepers). This is a much easier transition than going straight from 7 v 7 to 11 v 11. The advantages are as follows:

## Technical

- With fewer players on the pitch, each player has a greater number of ball contacts and so has more playing time and an increased demand on technical skills
- Players make more decisions and experience repeating game situations more often
- Technical speed is enhanced due to the size of the pitch
- Improved technical speed creates better tactical awareness
- Work rate and involvement are more consistent
- The technical/tactical ability of switching the point of attack occurs on a smaller pitch
- The smaller field dimensions and number of players on the field will require more concentration during transition (each time the ball changes hands)

## Physical

- Greater demands will be placed on fitness levels as levels of involvement/engagement are still at a premium
- The game will take on a quicker pace as there will be fewer interruptions and the ball will be in play more often
- Players will be in constant motion from penalty area to penalty area. There will be fewer long distance jogs and runs in straight lines
- The biggest demand will be on anaerobic fitness, as players will have to perform more short sprints
- The greatest improvement will be in soccer specific fitness

## Tactical

- With fewer players on a smaller pitch, players will be continually involved on both sides of the ball. In other words, they will be engaged in both defence and attack
- Players learn defence and attack, so become more well rounded and have a better understanding of the roles of other players
- 1-3-3-2 is probably the easiest system to play at this level
- It will encourage defenders to play out from the back, as they are only likely to be faced with two attackers. They must learn how to combine with the mid-field players to advance forwards and keep the shape
- It adds more flexibility to the system and allows players to interchange with each other through the various thirds of the field
- The extra striker creates the opportunity to teach the roles of the two central strikers. These players should learn how to combine with each other, play with back to goal and create space for forward runs from

the mid-field
- Other players can now learn to play off the strikers
- The technical/tactical possibilities are greater. Due to the smaller space, players are able to pass to any player on any part of the pitch, which improves perception
- U13 is considered the dawning of tactical awareness, although many players at this age still don't have the experience or maturity to execute team tactics. The more players there are on the field of play, the more complex the tactical situation becomes and the greater the impact on decision-making
- 11 v 11 often becomes a tactically overwhelming environment and since the problems are often too complex for some players to solve, they simply resort to just kicking the ball when it comes near them

## Psychological

- With fewer players the tactical situation is not as confusing. For many players at this age, their cognitive development is not at a stage where they can cope with the variables of 11 a-side
- With fewer players and a smaller pitch there will be a greater demand on mental focus (including anticipatory focus) as the game will always be nearer to them. This should help keep their attention
- With fewer players, it is easier to improve team work

When progressing from 7 v 7 to 9 v 9, it makes sense to add an extra midfield player and striker to the system. Immediately, the two extra players make the lines of defence, mid-field and attack more varied. Although more flexibility can now be added to the system, players should still be able to see the smaller inter-connecting shapes (mainly triangles, diamonds, squares, diagonals and lines) within the larger shape.

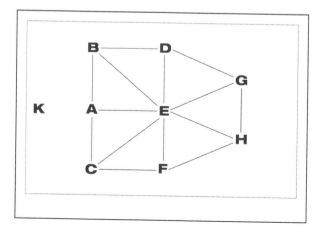

## Developing the 1-3-3-2 shape

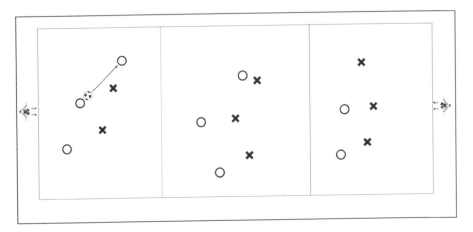

- Players stay in their own zones at the start in order to keep the team shape
- With only two attackers, the defenders should be able to play the ball out from the back
- Then allow transition between thirds. Players are allowed to move between zones, in order to create an overload in the middle third and equal numbers in the attacking third
- Once a team loses possession, the players that moved forward must drop back into their original starting zones
- **Progression**
- As above except when a team loses possession, any defensive player can move back to the original starting zone, as long as the correct balance is kept in each zone
- This will help develop greater vision, communication and team play and encourage the free movement of players throughout the field
- Players cease to become defenders, mid-field players or attackers but become total footballers instead

## Physical Development

The 13 to 14 age group can be a difficult time for developing children. Most are at the start of puberty and there can be massive changes in both the structures and functions of the body as they move from childhood to adolescence. Throughout puberty, the focus on movement efficiency and motor control must be maintained as the functional actions involving proprioception, motor coordination, flexibility and static and dynamic balance can be severely challenged during a growth spurt. What was once a simple exercise suddenly becomes challenging and players who showed precise control over their bodies and the ball will often lose coordination.

During a growth spurt, many gain strength and power but lose agility, coordination and suppleness. As soccer players this often means losing some control over the ball. If the technical foundation is not strong, then play ceases to be fluid and players quickly lose interest and often move to other sports that are easier to play. This is one reason why we must have a systematic programme in place, so that players get the necessary technical foundation prior to puberty.

Growth and maturation are specific to the individual and do not always follow chronological age. Biological age must therefore decide the training level and content. Soccer is a team sport and players from the same team can differ considerably in physique due to their individual speed of development. Coaches must be aware that some young people grow very quickly during puberty. They must therefore have a real understanding of the processes and characteristics of growth and maturation. This particular requirement of the coach's skill set is incredibly significant and yet often overlooked. The exercises and drills used by coaches must be programmed in a manner that recognises the individual needs of each child and their relative stage of development.

With so many changes taking place, a sensible approach at this level would be to reinforce actions already learnt and not introduce new material. Some skills might even have to be re-learned, so the coach should focus on re-patterning already familiar movements. Agility, balance and coordination should be practised, along with speed, strength, power, acceleration, deceleration, quick feet, reaction speed and flexibility. Dynamic balance should be challenged through ground-based activities and there should be a strong focus on body posture and muscle balance. All body alignments must be regularly checked, muscle balances corrected and optimum flexibility ranges maintained. Neurological development at this level will allow most players to use their fine motor skills, so practising with different sized balls is a useful way of monitoring progress.

Talent identification is not easy and coaches need far more than just an understanding of the skills of football. They must have knowledge of growth and maturation at this age and be able to develop individual programmes that take into account the impact of physiological changes. Unfortunately, decisions are often made by coaches during this level of development and as a consequence late maturing boys seem to be excluded from many team sports. With talent identification, coaches must understand that changes in growth and performance are highly individual. Unfortunately too many fail to understand this and it is often the early-maturing, taller, faster and stronger player who gets the recognition, rather than a late maturer of the same age. Many of the better performers in adulthood are often the late maturing youngsters but too often these players are missed and so lose heart and give up.

## Module Six (15 and 16 year olds)

In our programme players have progressed from 1 v 1 through 2 v 2, 3 v 3, 4 v 4, 5 v 5, 6 v 6, 7 v 7, 8 v 8 and 9 v 9 and at this stage most are now ready for 11 v 11. We strongly believe that this is a sound educational method for developing young soccer players, unlike the present system where players are forced into 11 v 11 matches before their bodies are physically mature enough to play the adult version of the game. To make things worse, most young players do not have an understanding of individual and group tactics, as they have not been coached in a developmental way. It therefore becomes very difficult for the coach to make tactical decisions, if they are not understood by the players.

At this level the coach must continue to emphasise the importance of ball possession and keeping the ball. The focus in training should therefore be on group skills and tactics, so much of the training sessions should still be dedicated to small-sided games such as 3 v 3, 4 v 4 and 6 v 6, as well as individual training with the ball. At 15 and 16 years of age players must also develop an understanding of the principles of attack and defence. In training the coach must teach depth, balance, delay and communication in defence and encourage width, mobility, penetration and improvisation in attack. Training must include functional play, team play and set plays but it must also be motivating and challenging and involve decision-making and transition play.

In moving towards the full game, advanced training should now place special emphasis on teaching team tactics, as well as reinforcing individual and group tactics. Players now need to experience and understand the importance and consequences of group and team tactics, building on the positional techniques and tactics they should already know. Using our systematic way of developing players, they have learned the basic elements of group and team tactics at a younger age, but now need to know how these elements relate to specific game situations and formations.

## Developing the 1-4-3-3 shape

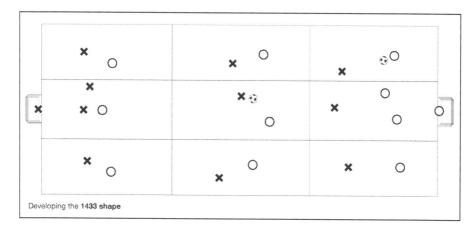

Developing the 1433 shape

- The pitch is divided into nine zones, as in the diagram, and teams play 11 v 11
- An attacker and defender are placed in each zone, apart from the central defensive zone where there are two defenders
- Have both teams with a ball each and playing through but not against each other
- When a rhythm has been established, make the game active
- Players must stay in their zones in order to keep the team shape

**Progression One**
Players can move zones but there must always be an attacker and defender in each zone and two defenders in the central defensive zone

**Progression Two**
- As above but withdraw one of the attackers into central mid-field and create a 1-4-4-2 situation
- When his team are attacking, one of the central mid-field players pushes into the attacking zone and creates a 1-4-3-3 situation
- When defending, the attacking mid-field player drops back into his defensive mid-field position

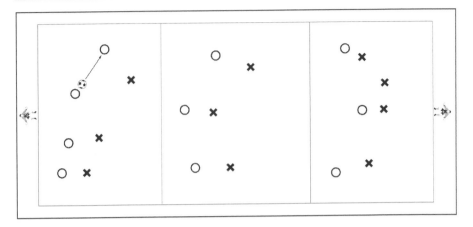

## Progression Three
- Create three zones and play 1 4 4 2
- Allow one player from each third to move into the next zone when attacking
- This will create an overload in mid-field and a 4 v 3 situation in attack
- Players change back to their original positions when defending
- This reinforces previous work on transitions between zones

## Progression Four
- Open up the zones and allow free play
- Can players keep their team shape without the help of the zones and thirds?

# Physical Development
The 15 to 16 age group can continue to be a difficult time for some children depending on their stage of development and coaches must constantly monitor changes in players' physiques. For some, growth in height becomes significantly greater, representing the start of puberty, whilst others have already gone through this stage at the previous level. This period often coincides with the adolescent growth spurt and the age at which the growth speed peaks is called the peak height velocity (PVH). There is a variation in the length of the growth spurt but it can last up to two years. The time of the start of the growth spurt gives information about the maturation of the child and the earlier the start, the more mature the child. Coaches must be able to monitor this in order to place early and late developers into their appropriate biological training groups and provide them with the correct training loads and competition.

The late developers will need to continue focusing on movement efficiency and motor control, as well as reinforcing many of their technical skills. An explanation of what is happening to them and why their movement skills may be adversely affected will help them understand that this is normal. However, for those who have gone through their PHV then big changes in training can now take place, with volume and intensity of work increasing.

## Strength

Twelve months after the end of the PHV is the ideal time for developing strength. Training should involve circuit training using own body weight plus whole body activities for developing the core. Athletically appropriate resistance challenges can be provided by dumbbells, medicine balls, viprs, kettlebells, tubing, sand and hills. These work the body in all three planes of movement and help develop the correct neural patterning required for competition. Functional activities can also be carried out on the pitch, which could involve a partner and include pushing and pulling on two legs and one leg, in order to improve coordination and balance as well as strength. A progressive plyometric programme, which should have been started at eight or nine years of age, is also essential if we wish to optimise the power performance of young players. However, due to differences in body size and maturity, it is important to look beyond a teenager's chronological age when developing a strength training programme.

## Speed

This is the third critical window for developing speed, which keeps increasing for boys until 18 years of age. Coaches should continue to work on speeding up the central nervous system but should also focus on developing the anaerobic alactic energy system. Interval training should be introduced along with linear, lateral and multi-directional speed work. Quickness, foot speed and explosive jumping power should be carried out all year round and be a regular part of the warm up.

## Flexibility

The flexibility of 15 and 16 year olds needs to be monitored carefully. Dynamic flexibility should always be used prior to practice or a game, as this can enhance performance. Static stretching should not be used prior to activity as research tells us it can be detrimental to performance. However, at this age a consistent static stretching programme after a practice or game is essential and can dramatically improve flexibility and reduce the risk of injury. The period of rapid growth can be a major risk factor for some adolescents, as the skeletal growth is not always matched by muscle and tendon growth, causing a decrease in flexibility. If there is time, a separate session devoted to stretching is recommended. If not, then players should be encouraged to carry out stretching sessions in their own time.

**Endurance**

For many children, after the onset of PHV, the major physiological systems that respond to training in adults respond in a similar fashion in children, although not always to the same degree. As a result, training in endurance can now take place. Intermittent aerobic training is ideal for improving endurance fitness and the training should be based on small-sided games and skill-based conditioning drills. As before, the players should be placed in groups according to biological maturation and not chronological age. The coach can adjust the rules, number of players per team, length of the game and size of the pitch according to ability levels and the biological age of the group.

## Chapter 8

# Introduction to the Games

We believe variable and random training is the way forward in youth foot-ball as it enables us to integrate the technical, tactical and physical simulta-neously. This will mean getting away from teaching technique in isolation and putting young players in practices which are close to the competitive situation of a real game. This is not to say that specific technical training or constant practice is not necessary, particularly when players are at the pre-control stage of learning. However, once players reach the constant and utilisation stages of development, then technique training should be prac-tised away from the training ground whenever possible. Alternatively, an individual who is experiencing a particular problem could be withdrawn from the session and be allowed to practise on his own before returning to the game. With the limited training time at our disposal, it is essential that young players start to understand time and space and are able to make a fast response to the situation they are in. In order to achieve this (and de-pending on their stage of development) it might be necessary to overload some games so that the players have every chance of success.

It is common sense that playing games with fewer players on smaller pitches is more appropriate when younger, before moving towards 11 v 11 when they are ready. However, training in 3 v 3 or 4 v 4 for under 18s is just as important as it is for the under 9s. All the coach has to do is increase the complexity of the game as the players develop. Practice games from 8 v 8 to 11 v 11 will improve playing ability, but players will only experience a few repetitions of any given situation, so eventually progress will stagnate as no new memory maps will be created. The only way to break the barrier is lots of practice in a variety of small-sided games, where similar situations keep on occurring. Examples of these reoccurring situations would be taking a first touch under pressure, receiving a variety of passes at differ-ent speeds and angles, shielding the ball, being aware of the next pass, switching play, closing down, running with the ball, defending as a group, attacking as a group, estimating the angle and distance between players, judging the position of team mates and the opposition and so on. We must vary the training according to the age and ability of the players, so that they continually have to deal with the types of situation suggested above.

Young players need to practise and repeat the same things in a variety of different ways. However, not only do they need to play small-sided games, they must also be exposed to many different learning environ-ments, thus varying the problems they have to solve. It is essential that we always involve the cortex of the brain as this is the part used in problem solving. Ensure they train on different surfaces including astro-turf, shale, grass, sand, slopes, uneven ground, muddy ground, long grass, short grass etc, in order to improve proprioception and tactile awareness. Play even teams, uneven teams, older players with younger players etc and change the shape of the pitch from wide to long and narrow, triangular, diagonal, diamond, circular and hexagon. It is essential that children are given different problems to solve whilst still practising the game, as this will involve their highest cortical brain. If the games are adapted to the age and ability of the children and presented in an imaginative and simple way, then the players will constantly be building up a picture of the game whilst learning to spot the cues. The game will now mean something and so more effective learning will take place, which should enable them make quicker and more accurate decisions.

Although it is necessary to move away from drills, it is equally important that players are not put into game situations that are too complicated and beyond their comprehension. A good example of this would be nine year olds playing 9 v 9 in a tight area or under 11s playing 11 v 11 on a full-size pitch. A lack of experience, strength and understanding would inevitably lead to poor perception, awareness and decision-making. In addition, an overload like this would simply cause the brain and enthusiasm to shut down.

Another major factor to consider is the player's field of vision, because most children only see the bigger picture when the ball is far away from them. As soon as a player is directly involved in the game, his field of vision gets smaller and he switches from a wide angle to a narrow angle view. Most nine year olds are not able to get out of this shrunken view until the play is over, because their attention is concentrated on the tunnel. Instead of refocusing vision for a brief second on the wider field of play, they remain in the tunnel and, under pressure, simply kick the ball anywhere, as they can't get their heads up. This is another major reason for playing a variety of small-sided games with fewer players on the field, as it enables the players to receive and control the ball with an open stance, which allows them to see the bigger picture. Playing in large-sided games, before they are ready, is counterproductive and game action speed simply slows down.

The games in the book have been divided into categories, with each group of games dedicated to a particular theme. The themes are: 1 v 1, maintaining possession, attacking a line or zone, attacking a target, defending from the front and switching games. The aim is that the set-up of the game will teach the particular theme that is being promoted. We have also added variations to most of the games and it will be down to the imagination of the coach to develop these further. It is essential that coaches are not frightened to experiment! However, they must start with a fundamental understanding of what they are trying to achieve in each session and have a clear vision of where the programme is going in the future. Small-sided games, played without a technical and tactical purpose, simply become an exercise in time- filling. Although this might be better than drills, without specific objectives, what is the player learning?

Most of the games in this book will benefit players who already demonstrate a basic grasp of soccer fundamentals and have reached the utilisation stage of learning. The age of the player is secondary for most of the games, although some of them will be far more than many young players can cope with. The job of the coach is to see where his players are in the cognitive developmental process and change the games accordingly. The task must always go from easy to difficult and simple to complex. The following are suggestions of how the games could be altered to suit the needs of the players.

## Size of the pitch

### Low Difficulty
The space of play is expanded according to the number of players on the pitch e.g. play 3 v 3 in a space of 25m x 25m.

### Medium Difficulty
The space of play is reduced according to the number of players on the pitch e.g. play 3 v 3 in a space of 20m x 20m.

### High Difficulty
The space of play is reduced according to the number of players on the pitch e.g. play 3 v 3 in a space of 15m x 15m

## Number of players

### Low Difficulty
When players have a low level of understanding and are at the control stage of learning, then play with superior numbers e.g. play 6 v 2 in an area of 20m x 20m. This makes it much easier to carry out offensive actions as players have more time to think.

### Medium Difficulty
When players have reached the utilisation stage of learning, it is now possible to play with even numbers e.g. 4 v 4 in a 25m square.

**High Difficulty**

When players have reached the proficiency stage of learning, it is now possible to play with smaller numbers e.g. 1 v 2 in a 10m square or 3 v 4 in a 20m square. This makes it far more difficult to carry out offensive actions as there is less time for attackers to think and easier for defenders to press the ball.

## Number of touches

**Low Difficulty** - free touches
**Medium Difficulty** - 3 touches
**High Difficulty** - 1 or 2 touches

## Number of passes to gain a point

**Low Difficulty**
Reduce the number of passes to win a point e.g. 4 to 6 passes.

**Medium Difficulty**
Increase the number of passes to win a point e.g. 6 to 8 passes.

**High Difficulty**
Increase the number of passes to win a point e.g. 9 or 10 passes.

Playing games which are appropriate for age and ability will help teach the basic concepts of attack and defence. Players will need to develop an understanding of the following tactics if they are to progress in football.

## Offensive Tactics
- Possession of the ball
- Width
- Support when in possession
- Wall passes
- Overload e.g. 2 v 1
- Change of direction
- Rhythm and change of rhythm
- Speed of play
- Depth of play
- Create, occupy and maintain space

## Defensive Tactics
- Positioning
- Interceptions

- Anticipation
- Cover
- Zone defence
- Man to man marking
- Pressing
- Retreat
- Reduce space

What is taught must therefore be match-related and the games in the book will achieve this aim. Guidelines are suggested for each game (size of pitch, number of players etc) but it will be down to the coach to change them according to the ability of those he is working with. The chart below gives a few variations of how the games could be adapted to suit the needs of the players.

- 3 v 1, 3 v 3 + 3, 3 v 3 + 2, 3 v 3 + 1, 3 v 3, 3 v 3 with limited touches, 3 v 3 man to man marking, 3 v 4

- 4 v 4 + 4, 4 v 4 + 2, 4 v 4 + 1, 4 v 4, 4 v 4 with limited touches, 4 v 4 man to man marking, 4 v 5

- 5 v 5 + 5, 5 v 5 + 2, 5 v 5 + 1, 5 v 5, 5 v 5 with limited touches, 5 v 5 man to man marking, 5 v 6

- 6 v 6 + 6, 6 v 6 + 2, 6 v 6 + 1, 6 v 6, 6 v 6 with limited touches, 6 v 6 man to man marking, 6 v 7

- 7 v 7 + 7, 7 v 7 + 2, 7 v 7 +1, 7 v 7, 7 v 7 with limited touches, 7 v 7 man to man marking, 7 v 8

Using 3 v 3 as an example, the following games demonstrate how coaches can gradually increase the complexity of the matches to meet the needs of his players. The same format could also be used with 4 v 4, 5 v 5, 6 v 6 and 7 v 7.

Game One

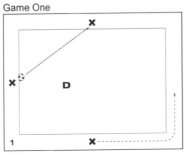

3 v 1 in a 5 metre square
The Xs can move around the
outside of the square but cannot
enter it.

Game Two

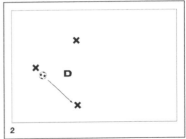

3 v 1 in a 10 metre square
Attackers can move anywhere
inside the square.

Game Three

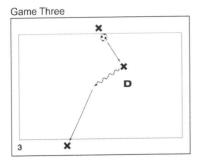

Play 3 v 1 in a 10m x 8m rectangle
The attacker in the middle zone tries
to work the ball from one end player
to the other and back. If the defender
wins the ball, he becomes the attacker.

Game Four

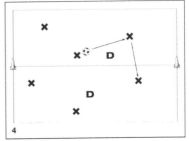

Play 3 v 1 in two 10m x 8m rectangles
Players must stay in their designated
half, including the defenders. The aim
is for the attackers to pass the ball from
one half to the other without losing
possession.

Game Five

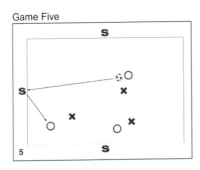

Play 3 v 3 + 3 in a 15m square. The
support players may move around the
outside of the square but must return the
ball to the team that passed to them.
The support players cannot be tackled.

Game Six

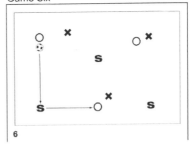

Play 3 v 3 + 3 in a 20m square. The support players move anywhere in the
square, play for the team in possession
and are restricted to two touches.

Game Seven

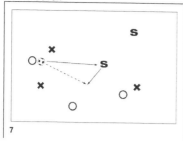

Play 3 v 3 + 2, in an 18m square. Teams score a point each time they successfully play a one-two with a support player.

Game Eight

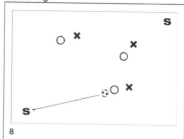

Play 3 v 3 + 2. The support players are placed in diagonally opposite corners and play for the team in possession. They cannot be tackled.

Game Nine

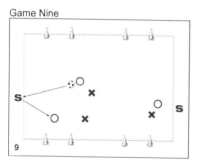

Play 3 v 3 + 2 in a 20m square. Each team attacks and defends two goals. Two support players are placed on either side of the pitch and play for the team in possession.

Game Ten

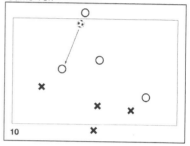

Play 3 v 3 + 2 in a 20 cm square. The support player stands behind his own goal-line and cannot be tackled. Teams score by crossing their opponent's goal-line with the ball. The outlet player must always make himself available to receive the ball.

Game Eleven

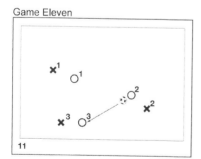

Play 3 v 3 in a 20m square. Players mark man to man and are only allowed to tackle the player they are assigned to. Score one point for five consecutive passes.

Game Twelve

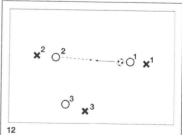

Play 3 v 3 in a 20m square. Players mark man to man and score a point for every takeover.

Game Thirteen

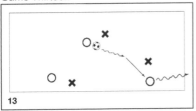

13

Play 3 v 3 in a 30m x 15m rectangle. Each team attacks and defends a 15m end line and scores by stopping the ball on the line. The shape of the pitch should encourage dribbling.

Game Fourteen

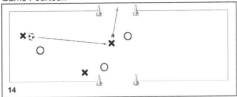

14

Play 3 v 3 in a 30m x 15m rectangle. Each team attacks and defends a 5m goal placed in the middle of each 30m line. The finish must be one touch. The shape of the pitch should encourage wing play and crossing.

Game Fifteen

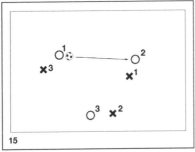

15

Play 3 v 3 in a 20m square. Players are numbered 1, 2 and 3 and score a point for every successful pass to the next player in the sequence. Therefore if 1 passes to 2, 2 passes to 3 or 3 passes to 1, that player scores a point. Players keep their own scores.

Game Sixteen

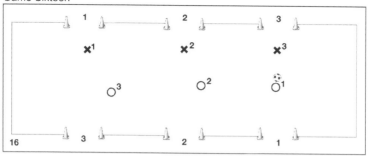

Play 3 v 3 in a 25m x 20m rectangle. Each team attacks and defends three goals.
This game gives attacking players targets to attack and defenders targets to protect.
When attacking, players can score in any goal. However, when defending, only X1 can de-
fend goal 1, X2 goal 2 and X3 goal 3. The same applies to the Os when they are defending.

In choosing a games-based approach, it is necessary to structure a series of
progressions, like the ones above, where players have lots of ball touches,
are given the opportunity to improve their passing and receiving skills, are
constantly moving, making tactical decisions and reacting to a stimulus.
The games must have a specific and defined focus, so that everything the
coach teaches is transferable to matches, which will help young players
learn when and why to use a particular skill. By conditioning the games
and using a variety of game-like activities to create a challenging environment, it is hoped the players will realise the importance of skill development when they see the need for it in real match situations. This might
encourage them to practise more with the ball, both on their own and
with friends. If the coach manages to achieve this and allows young players to apply their skills in endless match situations, then the game will truly
become the teacher!

○       Player

✖       Player

〜〜〜➤   Dribbling

- - - - - ➤   Player movement

———➤   Pass

➤———➤   Shot at Goal

⌂   Goal

K   Keeper

◭   Cone

⚽   Ball

**Key** to Illustrations

## Chapter 9

# 1 v 1, 2 v 2 and 3 v 3

## Exercise 1

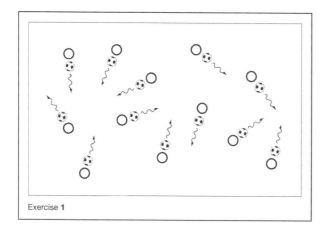

Exercise 1

**Equipment:** 4 cones, 12 balls    **No of players:** 12

**Time:** 12 sec x 6, with 30 sec recovery    **Pitch size:** 30m x 25m

**The Game:**
- Players work in a 30m x 25m grid with a ball each
- They dribble the ball at maximum speed, stopping and changing direction continually
- Players work for 12 seconds, then slowly dribble the ball for 30 seconds before repeating the action
- The fast dribble is carried out six times. Players are given two min' recovery time before repeating the action

**Progression**
- To make the practice more demanding, players dribble the ball whilst combining different movements
- In the dribbling sequence they can sit down and get up, jump to head an imaginary ball, roll forwards, roll backwards etc, all without losing control of the ball
- Dribble the ball whilst hopping on the standing foot, without the dribbling foot touching the ground

## Exercise 2

**Equipment:** 4 cones, 12 balls          **No of players:** 12

**Time:** 10 sec/15 sec/25 sec/30 sec x 8     **Pitch size:** 30m x 25m

**The Game:**
- Players work in a 30m x 25m grid, with a ball each
- They dribble at maximum speed, stopping and changing direction continually
- Players dribble the ball at pace for 10 seconds, then have 10 seconds' recovery
- Players dribble at pace for 15 seconds, then have 15 seconds' recovery
- Players dribble at pace for 25 seconds, then have 25 seconds' recovery
- Players dribble at pace for 30 seconds, then have 30 seconds' recovery
- All of this is repeated twice

**Progression**
- To make the practice more demanding, players dribble the ball whilst combining different movements
- In the dribbling sequence, they can sit down and get up, jump to head an imaginary ball, roll forwards, roll backwards etc, without losing control of the ball
- Dribble the ball whilst hopping on the standing foot, without the dribbling foot touching the ground

## Exercise 3

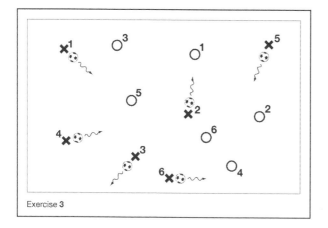

Exercise 3

**Equipment:** 4 cones, 6 balls          **No of players:** 12

**Time:** 12 sec x 6          **Pitch size:** 30m x 30m

### The Game:
- Players work in pairs, with one ball between them
- Player 1 dribbles the ball at maximum speed, stopping and changing direction continually
- After 12 seconds, he passes to his partner, who repeats the action
- This sequence is performed eight times by each player
- They then run slowly, passing the ball for two min before repeating the above sequence

### Progression
- To make the practice more demanding, players dribble the ball whilst combining different movements
- In the dribbling sequence, they can sit down and get up, jump to head an imaginary ball, roll forwards, roll backwards etc, without losing control of the ball
- To make players more visually aware, the player without the ball can copy the action carried out by the dribbling player e.g. if his partner sits down, then he repeats this action
- Dribble the ball whilst hopping on the standing foot, without losing control of the ball

## Exercise 4

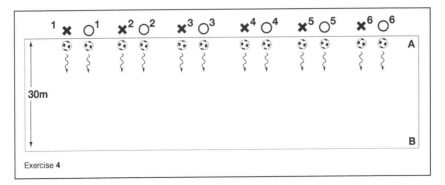

Exercise 4

**Equipment:** 4 cones, 12 balls

**Time:** 30 sec x 12

**No of players:** 12

**Pitch size:** 30m x 30m

**The Game:**
- Players work in pairs, with a ball each
- One of the pair is the offensive player and the other mirrors his actions
- The offensive player moves the ball from A to B whilst carrying out different touches, such as toe taps, step overs, Cruyff turns, quick accelerations and decelerations etc
- The partner has to keep his head up and copy and react to the moves of the offensive player
- After 30 seconds, change roles

**Progression**
- As above, except the offensive player dribbles anywhere in the grid, carrying out different touches, whilst his partner attempts to mirror his actions
- After 30 seconds, change roles

## Exercise 5

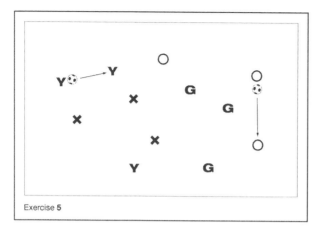

Exercise 5

**Equipment:** 4 cones, 2 balls     **No of players:** 12

**Time:** 3 min x 6     **Pitch size:** 40m x 25m

### The Game:
- Play two games of 3 v 3. Y's v X's and O's v G's
- The aim is to keep possession of the ball and complete as many passes as possible
- The players recover by running slowly and passing both balls for one minute
- The above sequence is repeated six times
- Players do not wear bibs as this will ensure the need for greater visual awareness

## Exercise 6

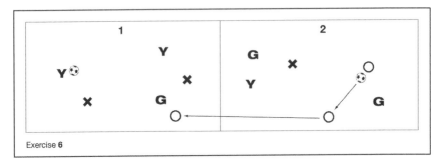

Exercise 6

**Equipment:** 6 cones, 2 balls, 6 bibs    **No of players:** 12

**Time:** 3 min x 8    **Pitch size:** 2 x 30m x 30m grid

**The Game:**

- Two games of 3 v 3 are played in the 60m x 30m double grid
- Y's v X's and O's v G's, with Y's and O's wearing bibs
- After three min, all players move into grid one
- Y's and O's combine as do X's and G's
- Teams play 6 v 6 in the smaller area
- Players can only intercept the ball and cannot tackle
- Work for three min, then change back to the two 3 v 3 games in the double grid
- Play four games of 3 v 3 and four games of 6 v 6

## Exercise 7

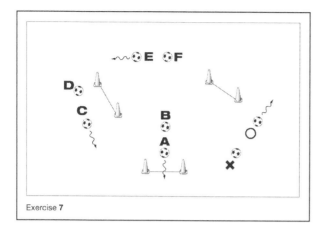

Exercise **7**

**Equipment:** 10 cones, 8 balls          **No of players:** 8

**Time:** 1 min x 8          **Pitch size:** 35m x 25m

**The Game:**
- Players have a ball each and work in pairs
- One of the pair is designated the chaser
- On a signal from the coach, the chaser dribbles his ball and tries to touch his partner on the shoulder, without losing control of the ball
- The player being chased can go through or around any of the marked goals
- How many times can the chaser touch his partner on the shoulder in one minute?
- Allow players 30 seconds recovery and then change roles

## Exercise 8

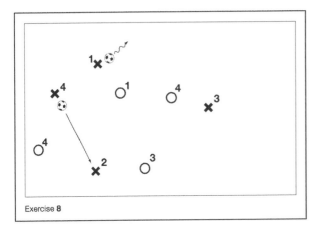

Exercise 8

**Equipment:** 4 cones, 2 balls          **No of players:** 8

**Time:** 4 min x 4          **Pitch size:** 30m square

### The Game:

- Divide the players into two teams of four, with one team wearing bibs
- Each player is given a number from 1 to 4
- Teams start off playing 4 v 4 until the coach shouts out "1's"
- The two 1's compete in a 1 v 1, whilst the other six players continue to play 3 v 3, all in the same area
- After a minute the coach shouts out "2's" and the two no 2's switch to playing 1 v 1, whilst the no 1's join the main group and carry on the 3v3
- This process continues until all the players have competed in a 1 v 1 against their opposite number
- After a minute's active recovery, the process starts again

## Exercise 9

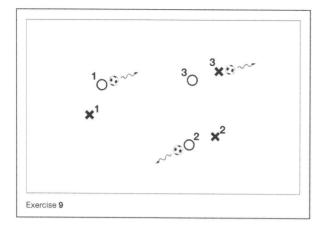

Exercise **9**

**Equipment:** 4 cones, 4 balls, 3 bibs      **No of players:** 6

**Time:** 5 min x 4                          **Pitch size:** 30m x 25m

### The Game:
- The players are divided into pairs, with one ball between two
- Each pair competes in a 1 v 1 for two min
- On a signal from the coach, a new ball is thrown in and the players combine to play 3 v 3
- After three min, players revert back to the original 1 v 1 situations
- This process is repeated four times

### Progression
At the end of each 3 v 3, players compete against a different opponent in the 1 v 1

## Exercise 10

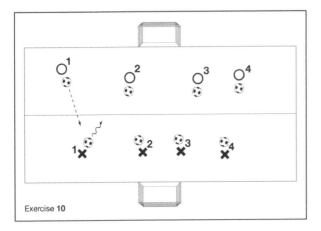

Exercise 10

**Equipment:** 2 goals, 6 cones, 8 balls    **No of players:** 8

**Time:** 4 min x 4    **Pitch size:** 2 x 30m x 25m grids

**The Game:**
- Divide the players into two teams of four
- Each player has a ball and is given a number from 1 to 4
- Players dribble the ball at pace in their own half of the field
- When the coach calls out a number e.g. O1, that player leaves his ball and sprints to close down his opposite number X1
- X1 immediately attacks O1, attempts to beat him and score in his opponent's goal
- If O1 wins the ball, he tries to score in X1's goal
- Players work for 30 seconds before the coach calls another number e.g. X3
- X3 leaves his ball and sprints to close down O3
- In the meantime, O1 and X1 return to their own half and continue dribbling their balls

**Progression 1**
- To maintain a high intensity, the coach calls out several numbers at the same time e.g. O2, X3, O4 and X1
- This will ensure a high level of activity, with four 1 v 1's going on simultaneously

**Progression 2**
Players try to maintain possession instead of shooting

## Exercise 11

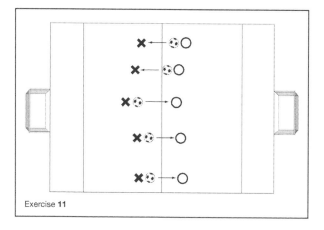

Exercise **11**

**Equipment:** 10 cones, 2 goals, 5 balls    **No of players:** 10

**Time:** 1 min x 10                          **Pitch size:** 30m x 25m

**The Game:**

- The players are divided into pairs, with one ball between two
- Players pass the ball quickly to each oth<uler on the spot
- On a signal from the coach, players compete in a 1 v 1, with O's attacking goal one and X's goal two
- If a player scores, he has to sprint back to the half way line, before he can rejoin the game
- All shots must be taken from within the 10m line
- Players compete for one minute, then return to the centre of the pitch and continue stationary passing
- After one minute's recovery, the pairs compete again

## Exercise 12

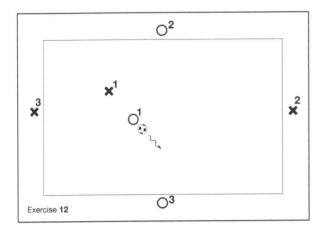

Exercise **12**

**Equipment:** 4 cones, balls          **No of players:** 6

**Time:** 1 min x 12          **Pitch size:** 10m square

**The Game:**
- Four neutral players stand on the sides of a square, as in the diagram
- They act as defenders and can move anywhere along their line
- The central pair (O1 and X1) compete in a 1 v 1
- The player with the ball attempts to maintain possession and dribble over any of the side lines, with the ball under control
- The defenders do their best to tackle him, without entering the field of play
- If successful, he turns and attacks any of the other lines
- At the same time, his opponent tries to win the ball and dribble over any of the side lines himself
- In order to maintain a high tempo, the coach should have plenty of balls available
- Work for one minute then change the central pair

## Exercise 13

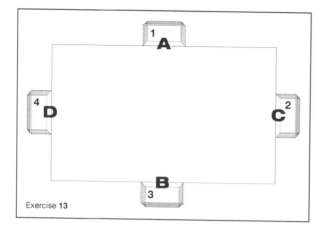

Exercise 13

**Equipment:** 4 cones, 4 goals, 2 balls  **No of players:** 4

**Time:** 2 min x 6  **Pitch size:** 20m square

**The Game:**
- A goal is placed on each side line of a 20m square, as in the diagram
- Two games of 1 v 1 take place simultaneously, A v B and C v D
- A defends goals 1 and 2 and attacks goals 3 and 4
- B defends goals 3 and 4 and attacks goals 1 and 2
- C defends goals 1 and 2 and attacks goals 3 and 4
- D defends goals 3 and 4 and attacks goals 1 and 2
- Work for two min then change the opponents and the goals that players attack and defend
- To make the game more chaotic, put another four players into the same square and play two more games of 1 v 1

## Exercise 14

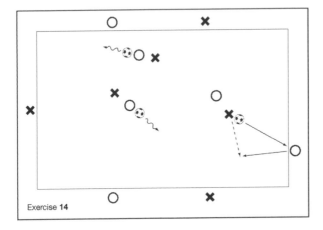

Exercise 14

**Equipment:** 4 cones, 3 balls          **No of players:** 12

**Time:** 1 min x 8          **Pitch size:** 20m square

**The Game:**
- Three pairs play 1 v 1 inside the square, as in the diagram
- Three more pairs are evenly distributed around the outside of the square and act as support players. They are limited to one touch
- The attackers try to maintain possession, with the help of the outside players
- Work for one minute then change roles with the outside players

**Progression 1**
Attackers can only use their own players on the outside

**Progression 2**
- The outside players jog slowly around the square, in an anti-clockwise direction
- This will encourage a greater accuracy of passing by the inside players

## Exercise 15

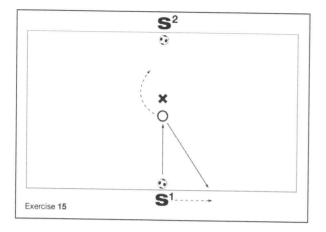

Exercise 15

**Equipment:** 4 cones, 2 balls          **No of players:** 4

**Time:** 45 sec x 8          **Pitch size:** 20m x 15m

**The Game:**
- Four players line up as in the diagram. The two support players are 20 metres apart and have a ball each
- O is the attacker and X the defender
- O calls and gets a pass from S1 and plays it back one touch
- He might spin and get a pass from S2 or another pass from S1. He always plays it back one touch
- X tries to intercept the passes. Even if successful, he gives the ball back and continues as the defender
- After 45 seconds, the attacker and defender change with the outside players

**Progression**
- As above, but only one ball is used
- O is the attacking player and starts with the ball
- His aim is to keep possession and make six consecutive passes with the outside players
- If X wins the ball, he attempts to do the same

## Exercise 16

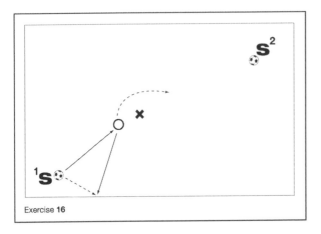

Exercise 16

**Equipment:** 4 cones, 2 balls          **No of players:** 4

**Time:** 45 sec x 8          **Pitch size:** 20m x 15m

### The Game:
- The four players line up, as in the diagram. The two support players have a ball each and are positioned in opposite corners of the grid
- O is the attacker and X the defender
- O calls and gets a pass from S1 and plays it back one touch
- He might spin and get a pass from S2 or another pass from S1
- X tries to intercept the passes. Even if successful, he gives the ball back and continues as the defender
- After 45 seconds, the attacker and defender change with the outside players

### Progression
- As above but only one ball is used
- O is the attacking player and starts with the ball
- His aim is to keep possession and make six consecutive passes with the outside players
- If X wins the ball he attempts to do the same

# Exercise 17

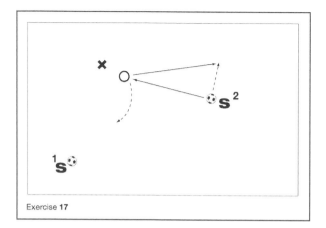

Exercise **17**

**Equipment:** 4 cones, 2 balls          **No of players:** 4

**Time:** 45 sec x 8          **Pitch size:** 20m x 15m

**The Game:**
- Four players line up as in the diagram. The two support players have a ball each and can move anywhere in the grid
- O is the attacker and X the defender
- O calls and gets a pass from S1 and plays it back one touch
- He might spin and get a pass from S2 or another pass from S1
- X tries to intercept the passes. Even if successful, he gives the ball back and continues as the defender
- After 45 seconds, O and X change roles with the support players

**Progression**
- As above but only one ball is used
- O is the attacking player and starts with the ball
- His aim is to keep possession and make six consecutive passes with the support players
- If X wins the ball he attempts to do the same

## Exercise 18

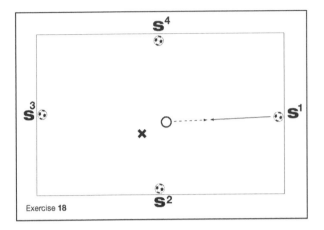

Exercise 18

**Equipment:** 4 cones, 4 balls

**No of players:** 6

**Time:** 45 sec x 12

**Pitch size:** 20m x 15m

**The Game:**
- Six players line up as in the diagram. The four support players have a ball each and can move anywhere along their lines
- O is the attacker and X the defender
- O calls and gets a pass from any of the support players. He immediately plays it back one touch
- X tries to intercept the passes. Even if successful, he gives the ball back and continues as the defender
- After 45 seconds, O and X change roles with two of the support players

**Progression**
- As above, but only one ball is used
- O is the attacking player and starts with the ball
- His aim is to keep possession and make six consecutive passes with the outside players
- If X wins the ball he attempts to do the same thing

*The following 20 games will follow the same format as Exercise 19 on the next page. Each game will start 1 v 1, progress to 2 v 2 and finish with 3 v 3. The number of players, time per interval and pitch size will be identical to those in Exercise 19, so from now on only the 1 v 1 games will be explained, as the 2 v 2 and 3 v 3 will be self-explanatory. At no stage do players wear bibs. This will encourage them to look for other cues and so improve their visual awareness.*

## Exercise 19

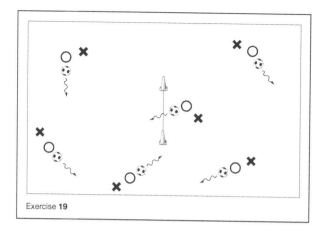

Exercise **19**

**Equipment:** 6 cones, 6 balls     **No of players:** 12

**Time:** 40 sec x 8, 2 min x 6, 3 min x 8     **Pitch size:** 30m x 25m

### The Game:
- Players work in pairs, with one ball between two
- Play 1 v 1 for 40 seconds
- The attacker's aim is to dribble across the six-metre line in the middle of the grid, with the ball under control
- The pairs recover by passing the ball whilst jogging

### Progression 1
- The pairs combine and play three games of 2 v 2 for two min
- The aim is for one of the attacking pair to dribble across the six-metre line in the middle of the grid, with the ball under control
- If successful, the pair has to pass the ball twice before they can attack the line again

### Progression 2
- Players combine and play two games of 3 v 3 for three min
- The aim is for the attacking team to keep possession and then dribble across the six-metre line in the middle of the grid, with the ball under control
- If successful, they have to pass the ball twice before they can attack the middle line again

## Exercise 20

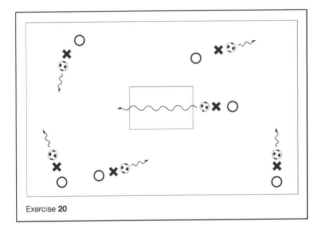

Exercise **20**

**Equipment:** 8 cones, 6 balls          **No of players:** 12

**Time:** 40 sec x 8, 2 min x 3, 3 min x 4          **Pitch size:** 30m x 25m

### The Game:
- Players work in pairs, with one ball between two
- Play 1 v 1 for 40 seconds
- The attacker's aim is to dribble across the five-metre square, with the ball under control
- The pairs recover by passing the ball whilst jogging

### Progression 1
- The pairs combine and play three games of 2 v 2 for two min
- The aim is for one of the attacking pair to dribble across the five-metre square, with the ball under control
- If successful, the pair has to pass the ball twice before they can attack the square again

### Progression 2
- Players combine and play two games of 3 v 3 for three min
- The aim is for the attacking team to keep possession and then dribble across the five-metre square, with the ball under control
- If successful, the trio has to make three passes before they can attack the square again

## Exercise 21

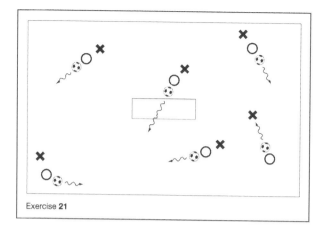

Exercise 21

**Equipment:** 8 cones, 6 balls          **No of players:** 12

**Time:** 40 sec x 8, 2 min x 6, 3 min x 4          **Pitch size:** 30m x 25m

### The Game:
- Players work in pairs, with one ball between two
- Play 1 v 1 for 40 seconds
- The attacker's aim is to dribble across the 5m x 2m rectangle, with the ball under control
- The pairs recover by passing the ball whilst jogging

### Progression 1
- The pairs combine and play three games of 2 v 2 for two min
- The aim is for one of the attacking pair to dribble across the 5m x 2m rectangle, with the ball under control
- If successful, the pair has to pass the ball twice before they can attack the rectangle again

### Progression 2
- Players combine and play two games of 3 v 3 for three min
- The aim is for the attacking team to keep possession and then dribble across the 5m x 2m rectangle, with the ball under control
- If successful, the trio has to make three passes before they can attack the rectangle again
- Players do not wear bibs

# Exercise 22

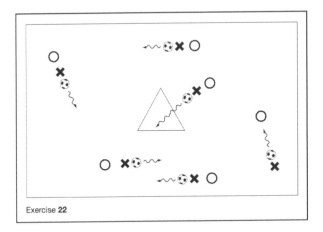

Exercise **22**

**Equipment:** 7 cones, 6 balls        **No of players:** 12

**Time:** 40 sec x 8, 2 min x 6, 3 min x 4        **Pitch size:** 30m x 25m

## The Game:
- Players work in pairs, with one ball between two
- Play 1 v 1 for 40 seconds
- The attacker's aim is to dribble across the 4m triangle, with the ball under control
- The pairs recover by passing the ball whilst jogging

## Progression 1
- The pairs combine and play three games of 2 v 2 for two min
- The aim is for one of the attacking pair to dribble across the triangle, with the ball under control
- If successful, the pair has to pass the ball twice before they can attack the triangle again

## Progression 2
- Players combine and play two games of 3 v 3 for three min
- The aim is for the attacking team to keep possession and dribble across the triangle, with the ball under control
- If successful, the trio has to make three passes before they can attack the triangle again
- Players do not wear bibs

## Exercise 23

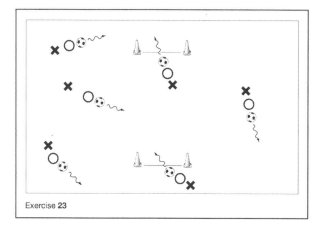

Exercise **23**

**Equipment:** 8 cones, 6 balls        **No of players:** 12

**Time:** 40 sec x 8, 2 min x 6, 3 min x 4    **Pitch size:** 30m x 25m

### The Game:
- Players work in pairs, with one ball between two
- Play 1 v 1 for 40 seconds
- The attacker's aim is to dribble across one of the 4m lines, with the ball under control
- The pairs recover by running slowly and passing the ball
- As a variation, Xs attack one line and Os the other
- The pairs recover by passing the ball whilst jogging

### Progression 1
- The pairs combine and play three games of 2 v 2 for two min
- The aim is for one of the attacking pair to dribble across either of the 4m lines, with the ball under control
- As a variation, Xs attack one line and Os the other

### Progression 2
- Players combine and play two games of 3 v 3 for three min
- The aim is for one of the attacking trio to dribble across either of the 4m lines, with the ball under control
- As a variation, Xs attack one line and Os the other

## Exercise 24

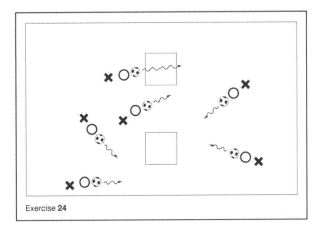

Exercise 24

**Equipment:** 12 cones, 6 balls          **No of players:** 12

**Time:** 40 sec x 8, 2 min x 6, 3 min x 4          **Pitch size:** 30m x 25m

**The Game:**
- Players work in pairs, with one ball between two
- Play 1 v 1 for 40 second
- The attacker's aim is to dribble across one of the 3m squares, with the ball under control
- As a variation, Xs attack one square and Os the other
- The pairs recover by passing the ball whilst jogging

**Progression 1**
- The pairs combine and play three games of 2 v 2 for two min
- The aim is for one of the attacking pair to dribble through either of the squares, with the ball under control
- As a variation, Xs attack one square and Os the other

**Progression 2**
- Players combine and play two games of 3 v 3 for three min
- The aim is for one of the attacking trio to dribble through either of the squares, with the ball under control
- As a variation, Xs attack one square and Os the other

# Exercise 25

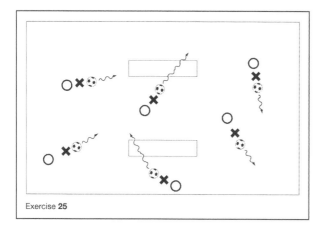

Exercise **25**

**Equipment:** 12 cones, 6 balls       **No of players:** 12

**Time:** 40 sec x 8, 2 min x 6, 3 min x 4       **Pitch size:** 30m x 25m

## The Game:
- Players work in pairs, with one ball between two
- Play 1 v 1 for 40 seconds
- The attacker's aim is to dribble across one of the 4m x 3m rectangles, with the ball under control
- As a variation, Xs attack one rectangle and Os the other
- The pairs recover by passing the ball whilst jogging

## Progression 1
- The pairs combine and play three games of 2 v 2 for two min
- The aim is for one of the attacking pair to dribble through either of the rectangles, with the ball under control
- As a variation, Xs attack one rectangle and Os the other

## Progression 2
- Players combine and play two games of 3 v 3 for three min
- The aim is for one of the attacking trio to dribble through either of the rectangles, with the ball under control
- As a variation, Xs attack one rectangle and Os the other

## Exercise 26

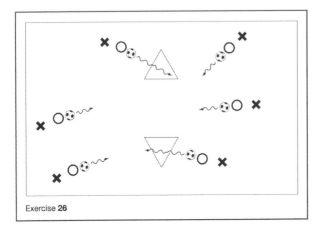

Exercise **26**

**Equipment:** 10 cones, 6 balls          **No of players:** 12

**Time:** 40 sec x 8, 2 min x 6, 3 min x 4          **Pitch size:** 30m x 25m

**The Game:**
- Players work in pairs, with one ball between two
- Play 1 v 1 for 40 seconds
- The attacker's aim is to dribble across one of the 4m triangles, with the ball under control
- As a variation, Xs attack one triangle and Os the other
- The pairs recover by passing the ball whilst jogging

**Progression 1**
- The pairs combine and play three games of 2 v 2 for two min
- The aim is for one of the attacking pair to dribble through either of the triangles, with the ball under control
- As a variation, Xs attack one triangle and Os the other

**Progression 2**
- Players combine and play two games of 3 v 3 for three min
- The aim is for one of the attacking trio to dribble through either of the triangles, with the ball under control
- As a variation, Xs attack one triangle and Os the other

## Exercise 27

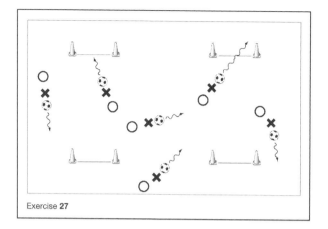

Exercise **27**

**Equipment:** 12 cones, 6 balls          **No of players:** 12

**Time:** 40 sec x 8, 2 min x 6, 3 min x 4          **Pitch size:** 30m x 25m

### The Game:
- Players work in pairs, with one ball between two
- Play 1 v 1 for 40 seconds
- Each player attacks and defends two small goals
- The attacker's aim is to dribble across one of the 3m goals, with the ball under control
- If he scores, he can then attack the other goal

### Progression 1
- The pairs combine and play three games of 2 v 2 for two min
- Each pair attacks and defends two small goals
- The aim is for one of the attacking pair to dribble through either goal, with the ball under control
- The pair can then attack the other goal

### Progression 2
- Players combine and play two games of 3 v 3 for three min
- The aim is for one of the attacking trio to dribble through either of the goals and then pass to a team mate
- If he dribbles through a goal, but does not pass to a team mate, then the goal does not count
- To make the game more difficult, allow teams to attack and defend diagonal goals

## Exercise 28

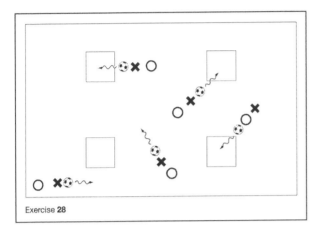

Exercise **28**

**Equipment:** 20 cones, 6 balls          **No of players:** 12

**Time:** 40 sec x 8, 2 min x 6, 3 min x 4      **Pitch size:** 30m x 25m

### The Game:
- Players work in pairs, with one ball between two
- Play 1 v 1 for 40 seconds
- Each player attacks and defends two small squares
- The attacker's aim is to dribble across one of the 2m squares, with the ball under control
- If he scores, he can then attack the other square

### Progression 1
- The pairs combine and play three games of 2 v 2 for two min
- Each pair attacks and defends two small squares
- The aim is for one of the attacking pair to dribble across either square, with the ball under control
- The pair can then attack the other square

### Progression 2
- Players combine and play two games of 3 v 3 for three min
- The aim is for one of the attacking trio to dribble through either of the squares and then pass to a team mate
- If he dribbles through a square, but does not pass to a team mate, then the goal does not count
- To make the game more difficult, allow teams to attack and defend diagonal squares

## Exercise 29

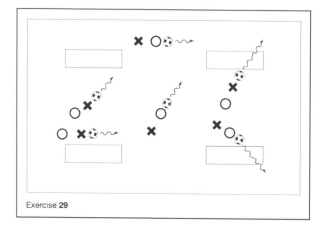

Exercise **29**

**Equipment:** 20 cones, 6 balls

**No of players:** 12

**Time:** 40 sec x 8, 2 min x 6, 3 min x 4

**Pitch size:** 30m x 25m

**The Game:**
- Players work in pairs, with one ball between two
- Play 1 v 1 for 40 seconds
- Each player attacks and defends two 4m x 2m rectangles
- The attacker's aim is to dribble across one of the rectangles, with the ball under control
- If he scores, he can then attack the other rectangle

**Progression 1**
- The pairs combine and play three games of 2 v 2 for two min
- Each pair attacks and defends two rectangles
- The aim is for one of the attacking pair to dribble through either rectangle, with the ball under control
- The pair can then attack the other rectangle

**Progression 2**
- Players combine and play two games of 3 v 3 for three min
- The aim is for one of the attacking trio to dribble through either of the rectangles and then pass to a team mate
- If he dribbles through a rectangle, but does not pass to a team mate, then the goal does not count
- To make the game more difficult, allow teams to attack and defend diagonal rectangle

## Exercise 30

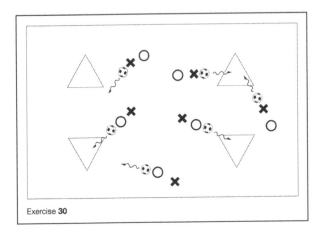

Exercise **30**

**Equipment:** 16 cones, 6 balls     **No of players:** 12

**Time:** 40 sec x 8, 2 min x 6, 3 min x 4     **Pitch size:** 30m x 25m

### The Game:
- Players work in pairs, with one ball between two
- Play 1 v 1 for 40 seconds
- Each player attacks and defends two small triangles
- The attacker's aim is to dribble across one of the 3m triangles, with the ball under control
- If he scores, he can then attack the other triangle

### Progression 1
- The pairs combine and play three games of 2 v 2 for two min
- Each pair attacks and defends two small triangles
- The aim is for one of the attacking pair to dribble through either triangle, with the ball under control
- The pair can then attack the other triangle

### Progression 2
- Players combine and play two games of 3 v 3 for three min
- The aim is for one of the attacking trio to dribble through either of the triangles and then pass to a team mate
- If he dribbles through a triangle, but does not pass to a team mate, then the goal does not count
- To make the game more difficult, allow teams to attack and defend diagonal triangles

## Exercise 31

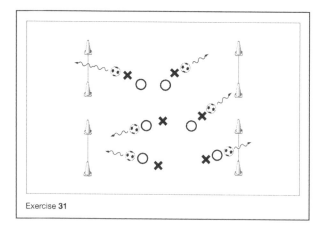

Exercise **31**

**Equipment:** 12 cones, 6 balls          **No of players:** 12

**Time:** 40 sec x 8, 2 min x 6, 3 min x 4          **Pitch size:** 30m x 25m

**The Game:**
- Players work in pairs, with one ball between two
- Play 1 v 1 for 40 seconds
- Each player attacks and defends two lateral goals
- The attacker's aim is to dribble across one of the 2m lateral goals, with the ball under control
- If he scores, he can then attack the other lateral goal

**Progression 1**
- The pairs combine and play three games of 2 v 2 for two min
- Each pair attacks and defends two lateral goals
- The aim is for one of the attacking pair to dribble across either lateral goal, with the ball under control
- The pair can then attack the other lateral goal

**Progression 2**
- Players combine and play two games of 3 v 3 for three min
- The aim is for one of the attacking trio to dribble through either of the lateral goals and then pass to a team mate
- If he dribbles through a lateral goal, but does not pass to a team mate, then the goal does not count
- To make the game more difficult, allow teams to attack and defend diagonal goals

## Exercise 32

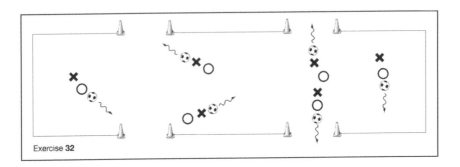

Exercise **32**

**Equipment:** 12 cones, 6 balls          **No of players:** 12

**Time:** 40 sec x 8, 2 min x 6, 3 min x 4          **Pitch size:** 30m x 25m

**The Game:**
- Players work in pairs, with one ball between two
- Play 1 v 1 for 40 seconds
- Each player attacks and defends two goals positioned on the end lines
- The attacker's aim is to dribble across one of the 2m goals, with the ball under control
- If successful, that player has to sprint back to his own goal line before he can rejoin the game

**Progression 1**
- The pairs combine and play three games of 2 v 2 for two min
- Each pair attacks and defends two goals
- The aim is for one of the attacking pair to dribble through either goal, with the ball under control
- If successful, both players have to sprint back to their own goal line before they can rejoin the game

**Progression 2**
- Players combine and play two games of 3 v 3 for three min
- The aim is for one of the attacking trio to dribble through either goal, and then pass to a team mate
- If successful, all three players have to sprint back to their own goal line before they can rejoin the game

## Exercise 33

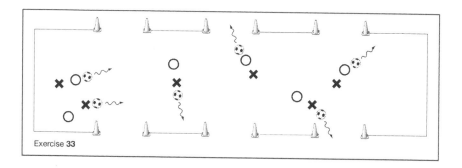

Exercise 33

**Equipment:** 16 cones, 6 balls      **No of players:** 12

**Time:** 40 sec x 8, 2 min x 6, 3 min x 4     **Pitch size:** 30m x 25m

### The Game:
- Players work in pairs, with one ball between two, and play 1 v 1 for 40 seconds
- Each player attacks and defends three goals, which have been placed on the end lines
- The attacker's aim is to dribble through one of the two-metre goals, with the ball under control
- If successful, that player has to sprint back to his own goal line before he can rejoin the game

### Progression 1
- The pairs combine and play three games of 2 v 2 for two min
- Each pair attacks and defends three goals
- The aim is for one of the attacking pair to dribble through a goal, with the ball under control
- If successful, both players have to sprint back to their own goal line before they can rejoin the game

### Progression 2
- Players combine and play two games of 3 v 3 for three min
- The aim is for one of the attacking trio to dribble through a goal, with the ball under control
- If successful, all three players have to sprint back to their own goal line before they can rejoin the game

## Exercise 34

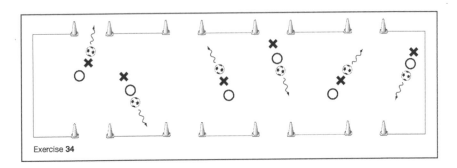

Exercise **34**

**Equipment:** 20 cones, 6 balls      **No of players:** 12

**Time:** 40 sec x 8, 2 min x 6, 3 min x 4      **Pitch size:** 30m x 25m

### The Game:
- Players work in pairs, with one ball between two, and play 1 v 1 for 40 seconds
- Each player attacks and defends four small goals, which have been placed on the end lines
- The attacker's aim is to dribble through one of the two-metre goals, with the ball under control
- If successful, that player has to sprint back to his own goal line before he can rejoin the game

### Progression 1
- The pairs combine and play three games of 2 v 2 for two min
- Each pair attacks and defends four goals
- The aim is for one of the attacking pair to dribble through a goal, with the ball under control
- If successful, both players have to sprint back to their own goal line before they can rejoin the game

### Progression 2
- Players combine and play two games of 3 v 3 for three min
- The aim is for one of the attacking trio to dribble through a goal, with the ball under control
- If successful, all three players have to sprint back to their own goal line before they can rejoin the game

## Exercise 35

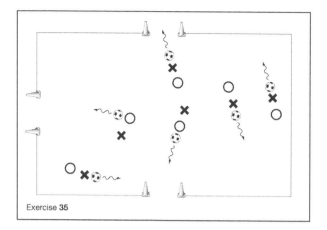

Exercise **35**

**Equipment:** 10 cones, 6 balls      **No of players:** 12

**Time:** 40 sec x 8, 2 min x 6, 3 min x 4      **Pitch size:** 30m x 25m

**The Game:**
- Players work in pairs, with one ball between two, and play 1 v 1 for 40 seconds
- Each player attacks and defends three small goals, which have been placed on three side lines
- The attacker's aim is to dribble through one of the two-metre goals, with the ball under control
- If successful, that player can now attack either of the other two goals

**Progression 1**
- The pairs combine and play three games of 2 v 2 for two min
- Each pair attacks and defends the three neutral goals
- The aim is for one of the attacking pair to dribble through a goal, with the ball under control
- If successful, that pair can now attack either of the other two goals

**Progression 2**
- Players combine and play two games of 3 v 3 for three min
- The aim is for one of the attacking trio to dribble through a goal, with the ball under control
- If successful, that trio can now attack either of the other two goals

## Exercise 36

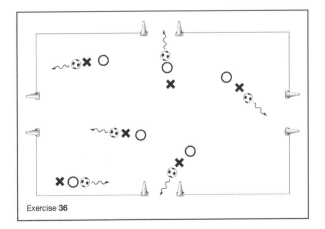

Exercise **36**

**Equipment:** 12 cones, 6 balls          **No of players:** 12

**Time:** 40 sec x 8, 2 min x 6, 3 min x 4      **Pitch size:** 30m x 25m

### The Game:
- Players work in pairs, with one ball , and play 1 v 1 for 40 seconds
- Each player attacks and defends four goals, one on each side line
- The attacker's aim is to dribble through one of the two-metre goals, with the ball under control
- If successful, that player can now attack any of the other goals
- As an alternative, each player can be assigned two goals to attack and two to defend

### Progression 1
- The pairs combine and play three games of 2 v 2 for two min
- Each pair attacks and defends the four neutral goals
- The aim is for one of the attacking pair to dribble through a goal, with the ball under control
- If successful, that pair can now attack any of the other goals
- As an alternative, each pair can be assigned two goals to attack and two to defend

### Progression 2
- Players combine and play two games of 3 v 3 for three min
- The aim is for one of the attacking trio to dribble through a goal, with the ball under control
- If successful, that trio can now attack any of the other goals
- As an alternative, each trio is assigned two goals to attack and two to defend

# Exercise 37

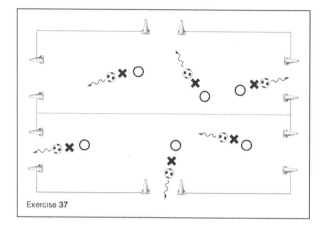

Exercise **37**

**Equipment:** 18 cones, 6 balls          **No of players:** 12

**Time:** 40 sec x 8, 2 min x 6, 3 min x 4          **Pitch size:** 30m x 25m

## The Game:
- Players work in pairs, with one ball between two, and play 1 v 1 for 40 seconds
- Each player attacks and defends three small goals, placed as shown in the diagram
- The attacker's aim is to dribble through one of the two-metre goals, with the ball under control
- If successful, he has to sprint back to the half-way line before he can rejoin the game

## Progression 1
- The pairs combine and play three games of 2 v 2 for two min
- Each pair attacks and defends the three small goals, placed as shown
- The aim is for one of the attacking pair to dribble through a goal, with the ball under control
- If successful, that pair has to sprint back to the half-way line before they can rejoin the game

## Progression 2
- Players combine and play two games of 3 v 3 for three min
- The aim is for one of the attacking trio to dribble through a goal, with the ball under control
- If successful, the trio has to sprint back to the half-way line before they can rejoin the game

## Exercise 38

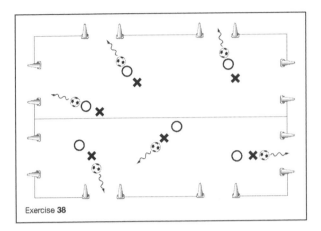

Exercise 38

**Equipment:** 22 cones, 6 balls      **No of players:** 12

**Time:** 40 sec x 8, 2 min x 6, 3 min x 4      **Pitch size:** 30m x 25m

**The Game:**
- Players work in pairs, with one ball between two, and play 1 v 1 for 40 seconds
- Each player attacks and defends four small goals, placed as shown in the diagram
- The attacker's aim is to dribble through one of the two-metre goals, with the ball under control
- If successful, he has to sprint back to the half-way line before he can rejoin the game

**Progression 1**
- The pairs combine and play three games of 2 v 2 for two min
- Each pair attacks and defends the four small goals, placed as shown
- The aim is for one of the attacking pair to dribble through any of the four goals, with the ball under control
- If successful, that pair has to sprint back to the half-way line before they can rejoin the game

**Progression 2**
- Players combine and play two games of 3 v 3 for three min
- The aim is for one of the attacking trio to dribble through a goal, with the ball under control
- If successful, the trio has to sprint back to the half-way line before they can rejoin the game

## Exercise 39

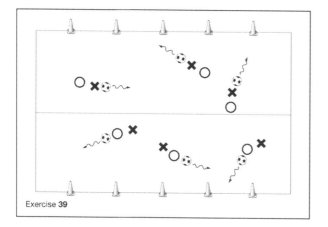

Exercise **39**

**Equipment:** 16 cones, 6 balls          **No of players:** 12

**Time:** 40 sec x 8, 2 min x 6, 3 min x 4          **Pitch size:** 30m x 25m

### The Game:
- Players work in pairs, with one ball between two, and play 1 v 1 for 40 seconds
- Each player attacks and defends five cones, which are spaced evenly along both end lines, as shown in the diagram
- The attacker's aim is to strike or knock over one of the cones
- If successful, he has to sprint back to the half-way line before he can rejoin the game
- As an alternative, the attacker could dribble around a cone rather than strike it

### Progression 1
- The pairs combine and play three games of 2 v 2 for two min
- Each pair attacks and defends five cones, placed as shown
- The attacker's aim is to strike or knock over one of the cones
- If successful, that pair has to sprint back to the half-way line before they can rejoin the game
- As an alternative, an attacker could dribble around the cone rather than strike it

### Progression 2
- Players combine and play two games of 3 v 3 for three min
- The aim is for one of the attacking trio to strike a cone placed on the end line

- If successful, the trio has to sprint back to the half-way line before they can rejoin the game
- As an alternative, an attacker could dribble around the cone rather than strike it

## Exercise 40

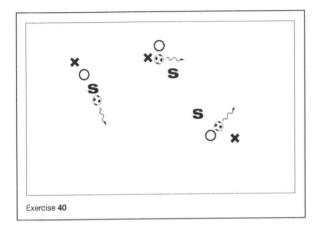

Exercise 40

**Equipment:** 4 cones, 3 balls          **No of players:** 9

**Time:** 1 min x 10          **Pitch size:** 20m square

### The Game:
- Three groups play 1 v 1 v 1
- The player in possession tries to keep the ball by feinting, beating his opponents and shielding it
- Work for one minute then allow players an active recovery
- A different player starts with the ball at the beginning of each new game

## Exercise 41

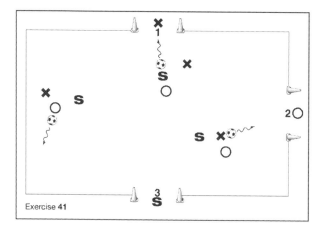

Exercise **41**

**Equipment:** 10 cones, 3 balls          **No of players:** 9

**Time:** 1 min x 10          **Pitch size:** 20m square

**The Game:**
- Three two-metre goals are placed on three sides of the square, as in the diagram
- Three groups play 1 v 1 v 1. Each player is given a goal to defend and two to attack
- In the diagram, X's defend goal 1 and attack goals 2 and 3, O's defend goal 2 and attack goals 1 and 3 and S's defend goal 3 and attack goals 1 and 2
- The attacking player scores a point if he can dribble through one of his opponents' goals, with the ball under control
- The player whose goal has been scored in starts with the ball
- A different player starts with the ball at the beginning of each new game

**Progression**
The three goals now become neutral and players can attack, defend and score in any of them

## Exercise 42

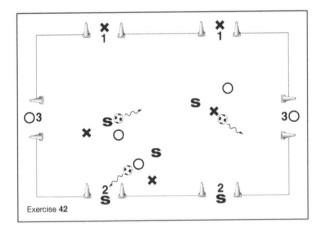

Exercise 42

**Equipment:** 16 cones, 3 balls

**Time:** 1 min x 10

**No of players:** 9

**Pitch size:** 25m x 20m

### The Game:
- Six two-metre goals are placed on four sides of the grid, as in the diagram
- Three groups play 1 v 1 v 1. Each player is given two goals to defend and four to attack.
- In the diagram, X's defend the no 1 goals and attack goals 2 and 3, S's defend no 2 goals and attack goals 1 and 3 and O's defend no 3 goals and attack goals 1 and 2
- The attacking player scores a point if he can dribble through one of his opponents' goals, with the ball under control
- The player whose goal has been scored in starts with the ball
- A different player starts with the ball at the beginning of each new game

### Progression
The six goals now become neutral and players can attack, defend and score in any of them

## Exercise 43

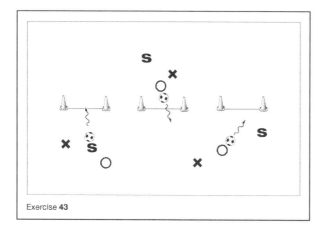

Exercise **43**

**Equipment:** 10 cones, 3 balls    **No of players:** 9

**Time:** 1 min x 10    **Pitch size:** 25m x 20m

### The Game:
- Three neutral goals, each three metres wide, are placed in the centre of the grid, as in the diagram
- Three groups play 1 v 1 v 1
- The player in possession tries to beat his opponents and dribble through any of the goals, with the ball under control
- He scores a point every time he is successful
- A different player starts with the ball at the beginning of each new game

## Exercise 44

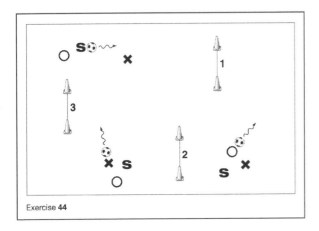

Exercise 44

**Equipment:** 10 cones, 3 balls          **No of players:** 9

**Time:** 1 min x 10          **Pitch size:** 25m x 20m

**The Game:**
- Three lateral goals, each four metres wide, are placed on the pitch, as in the diagram
- Three groups play 1 v 1 v 1
- Each player is given a goal to defend and two to attack
- In the diagram, X's defend goal 1 and attack goals 2 and 3, O's defend goal 2 and attack goals 1 and 3 and S's defend goal 3 and attack goals 1 and 2
- The player in possession tries to beat his opponents and dribble through either of their goals, with the ball under control
- He scores a point every time he is successful
- A different player starts with the ball at the beginning of each new game

**Progression**
The three goals now become neutral and players can attack, defend and score in any of them

## Exercise 45

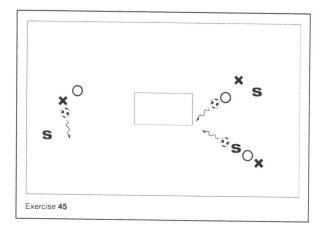

Exercise **45**

**Equipment:** 8 cones, 3 balls          **No of players:** 9

**Time:** 1 min x 10          **Pitch size:** 25m x 20m

### The Game:
- A five-metre square is placed in the middle of the grid, as in the diagram
- Three groups play 1 v 1 v 1
- The player with the ball tries to maintain possession, beat his opponents and dribble through the middle square, with the ball under control
- Every time he is successful, he scores a point
- A different player starts with the ball at the beginning of each new game

## Exercise 46

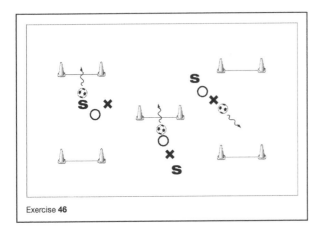

Exercise **46**

**Equipment:** 14 cones, 3 balls          **No of players:** 9

**Time:** 1 min x 10          **Pitch size:** 25m x 20m

**The Game:**
- Five goals, each two metres, wide are placed in the grid, as in the diagram
- Three groups play 1 v 1 v 1
- The five goals are neutral and players can attack, defend and score in any of them
- A player scores a point if he dribbles through a goal, with the ball under control
- A different player starts with the ball at the beginning of each new game

## Exercise 47

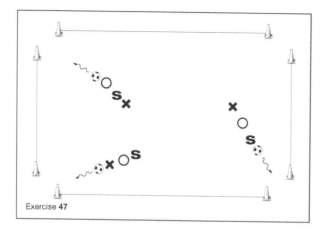

Exercise 47

**Equipment:** 12 cones, 3 balls     **No of players:** 9

**Time:** 1 min x 10     **Pitch size:** 25m square

### The Game:
- Four two-metre goals are placed in each corner of the square, as in the diagram
- Three groups play 1 v 1 v 1
- The four goals are neutral and players can attack, defend and score in any of them
- A player scores a point if he dribbles through a goal, with the ball under control
- A different player starts with the ball at the beginning of each new game

## Exercise 48

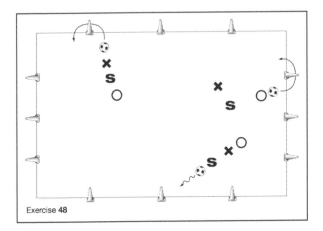

Exercise 48

**Equipment:** 12 cones, 3 balls    **No of players:** 9

**Time:** 1 min x 10    **Pitch size:** 25m square

### The Game:
- Twelve cones are placed around the outside of the square, as in the diagram
- Three groups play 1 v 1 v 1
- All the cones are neutral and players can attack and defend any of them
- A player scores a point if he dribbles around an outside cone, with the ball under control
- A different player starts with the ball at the beginning of each new game

Chapter 10

# Maintaining Possession

### Exercise 49

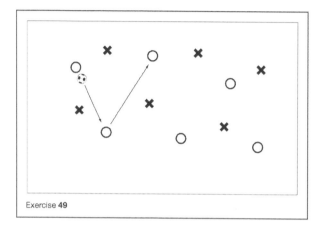

Exercise **49**

**Equipment:** 4 cones, set of bibs, balls

**No of players:** 12

**Time:** 4-8 x 6 min with 2 min recovery

**Pitch size:** 35m square

**The Game:**
- Play 6 v 6
- The attacking team tries to keep possession and complete five consecutive passes
- If successful, they earn a point

**Progression**
Teams play man to man marking and may only tackle the player they have been assigned to

## Exercise 50

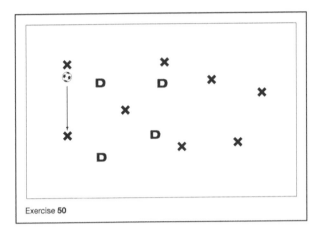

Exercise **50**

**Equipment:** 4 cones, 2 sets of bibs, balls

**No of players:** 12

**Time:** 4-8 x 6 min with 2 min recovery

**Pitch size:** 30m x 25m

**The Game:**
- Play 8 v 4. A team of eight players tries to maintain possession against four defenders
- If the defenders win the ball, they return it to the attackers

**Progression 1**
If the defenders win the ball, they try to pass to the coach, who is moving on the outside of the grid

**Progression 2**
If the defenders win the ball, they try to dribble to the outside of the grid, with the ball under control

## Exercise 51

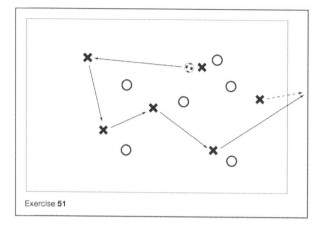

Exercise **51**

**Equipment:** 4 cones, set of bibs, balls          **No of players:** 12

**Time:** 3-8 x 6 min with 2 min recovery          **Pitch size:** 40m x 25m

**The Game**:
- Play 6v 6. The attacking team tries to maintain possession of the ball
- After five consecutive passes, they can attempt to pass to a player who has made a run outside the field of play
- If the pass is accurate and the receiving player controls the ball, then the team wins a point

## Exercise 52

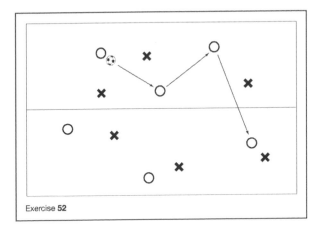

Exercise 52

**Equipment:** 6 cones, set of bibs, balls

**No of players:** 12

**Time:** 3-6 x 6 min with 2 min recovery

**Pitch size:** 40m x 30m

### The Game:
- Play 6 v 6. The field is divided into two zones (20m by 30m)
- There are three players from each team in the two zones
- The attacking team tries to maintain possession of the ball and after three passes may play to a team mate in the opposite zone
- Here the action is repeated. The ball cannot be transferred back until three consecutive passes have been completed

## Exercise 53

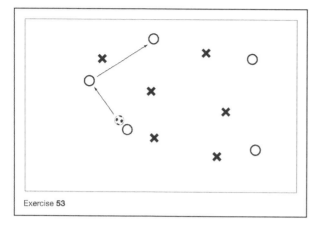

Exercise **53**

**Equipment:** 4 cones, set of bibs, balls     **No of players:** 11

**Time:** 4-8 x 5 min with 2 min recovery     **Pitch size:** 40m x 30m

**The Game:**
- Play 5 v 6. The team with inferior numbers attempts to keep the ball. Each player has unlimited touches
- If the team with superior numbers wins the ball, they also attempt to keep the ball, but are restricted to two touches
- After every five-minute game, change the teams so that all players experience both roles

## Exercise 54

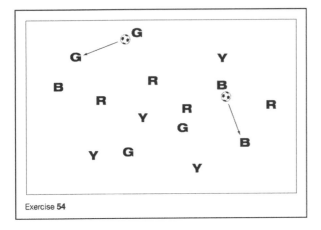

Exercise **54**

**Equipment:** 4 cones, 4 sets of bibs, balls    **No of players:** 16

**Time:** 3-6 x 8 min with 2 min recovery    **Pitch size:** 40m x 35m

**The Game:**
- Play 4 v 4 plus 4 v 4
- Red and blue play against each other and green and yellow play against each other, but with both games taking place on the same pitch
- Each team tries to keep possession of the ball and complete six consecutive passes
- If successful, they win a point
- Change opponents every eight minutes

## Exercise 55

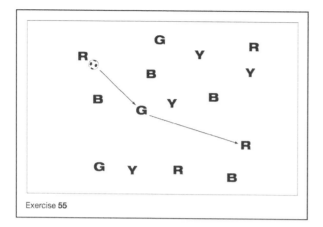

Exercise **55**

**Equipment:** 4 cones, 4 sets of bibs, balls     **No of players:** 16

**Time:** 3-6 x 8 min with 2 min recovery     **Pitch size:** 40m x 35m

**The Game:**
- Play 8 v 8. Red and green combine as one team and play against blue and yellow
- Each team tries to maintain possession of the ball and complete eight consecutive passes
- If successful, they gain a point
- Change opponents every eight minutes

**Progression**
- One colour has unlimited touches, whilst the other is restricted to two-touch i.e. red unlimited, green two-touch, yellow unlimited, blue two-touch
- The ball has to be passed in sequence i.e. red to green to red or blue to yellow to blue etc and this will immediately halve the passing options
- This is a difficult exercise and should only be used with more advanced players

## Exercise 56

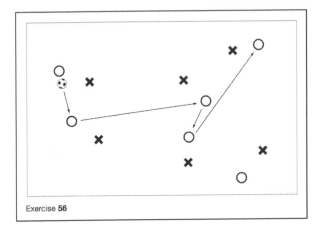

Exercise 56

**Equipment:** 4 cones, set of bibs, balls    **No of players:** 12

**Time:** 4-8 x 6 min with 2 min recovery    **Pitch size:** 40m square

### The Game:
- Play 6 v 6
- Each team has two players who pass the ball long (over 10 metres) and four players who pass the ball short (under 10 metres)
- The attacking team tries to keep possession of the ball but has to continually change its rhythm of passing from short to long
- Keep changing the role of the players, so that they get the chance to play short and long

## Exercise 57

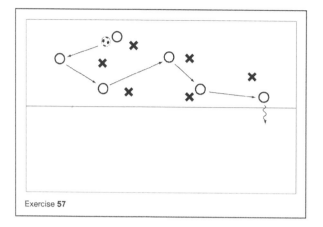

Exercise **57**

**Equipment:** 4 cones, set of bibs, balls    **No of players:** 12

**Time:** 4-8 x 6 min with 2 min recovery    **Pitch size:** 40m x 30m

**The Game:**
- Play 6 v 6. The field is divided into two zones (20m by 30m)
- The attacking team tries to maintain possession of the ball
- After five consecutive passes, they try to dribble or pass the ball into the second zone and maintain possession there
- An attacking player cannot wait in the second zone!
- The team wins a point for five consecutive passes in both zones

## Exercise 58

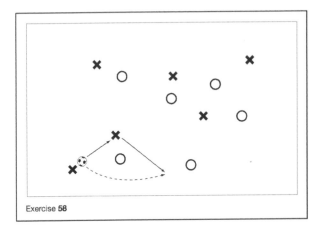

Exercise 58

**Equipment:** 4 cones, set of bibs, balls     **No of players:** 12

**Time:** Variable, 2 min recovery between games   **Pitch size:** 30m x 20m

**The Game:**
- Play 6 v 6. Each team tries to keep possession of the ball and complete as many 1/2s as possible
- Two coaches are needed to count the 1/2s for each team
- The first team to reach 20 1/2s is the winner

**Progression**
The first team to reach 20 takeovers, drag backs, or successful one-touch passes is the winner

## Exercise 59

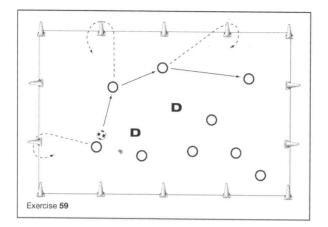

Exercise 59

**Equipment:** 8 cones, set of bibs, balls

**No of players:** 12

**Time:** 6-8 x 3 min plus 1 min recovery

**Pitch size:** 30m x 20m

### The Game:
- Play 10 v 2. After passing the ball, the player sprints around one of the outside cones and rejoins the game
- Players are limited to two touches
- Look for quick movement after the pass
- Change the defenders every three min

### Progression
Ask for different movements around the cones i.e. run backwards, jump over and turn 180 degrees, quick feet, spin behind etc

## Exercise 60

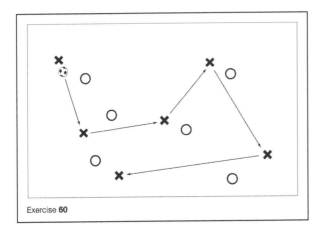

Exercise **60**

**Equipment:** 4 cones, set of bibs, balls

**No of players:** 12

**Time:** 4-8 x 6 min with 2 min recovery

**Pitch size:** 40m square

**The Game**:
- Play 6 v 6. The attacking team tries to maintain possession of the ball and complete five consecutive passes
- They score a point if the fifth pass is chipped to a team member and is caught
- If the ball is dropped, then the point does not count

**Progression**
- The fifth pass is chipped to a team member, who controls the ball and then catches it
- This is a difficult game and should only be used by more advanced players

## Exercise 61

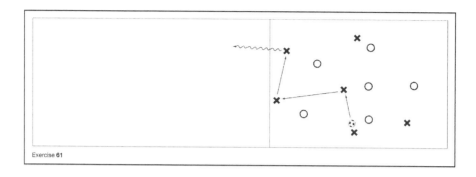

Exercise 61

**Equipment:** 6 cones, set of bibs, balls

**No of players:** 12

**Time:** 4-8 x 6 min with 2 min recovery

**Pitch size:** Pitch 1 30m x 30m
Pitch 2 60m x 30m

**The Game:**
- Play 6 v 6. The attacking team tries to maintain possession in the small square
- On the coach's signal, the teams move quickly into the larger area and carry on competing as before
- When the coach calls "change", the team in possession has responsibility for bringing the ball into the new area
- The opposition cannot challenge whilst this is happening
- After a few min, when the coach gives the signal, play is brought back to the smaller area by the team in possession and the game continues

## Exercise 62

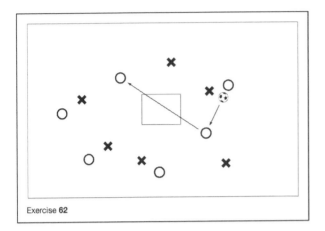

Exercise **62**

**Equipment:** 8 cones, set of bibs, balls    **No of players:** 12

**Time:** 4-6 x 6 min with 2 min recovery    **Pitch size:** 40m sq + 10m sq

**The Game:**
- Play 6 v 6. The attacking team tries to maintain possession of the ball
- They may play across the marked zone (10m by 10m) but must not enter it
- A team scores a point for six consecutive passes
- At least one of those passes must cross the marked zone

**Progression**
Players may enter the marked zone but the ball must not cross it

## Exercise 63

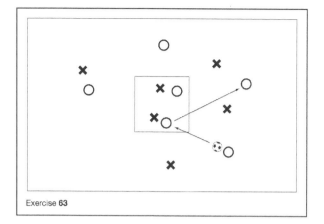

Exercise **63**

**Equipment:** 8 cones, set of bibs, balls          **No of players:** 12

**Time:** 6 x 8 min with 2 min recovery          **Pitch size:** 40m square

### The Game:
- Play 6 v 6
- Two players from each team are placed in the central zone (15m by 15m) and four in the outside zone
- Players must stay in their respective zones
- The attacking team tries to maintain possession of the ball and scores a point for six consecutive passes

### Progression
The ball has to be passed in sequence i.e. from the inside zone to the outside zone and back to the inside zone

## Exercise 64

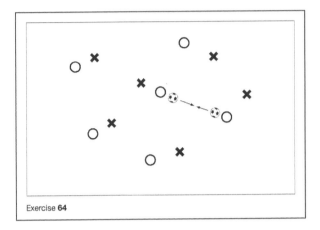

Exercise **64**

**Equipment:** 4 cones, 2 balls          **No of players:** 12

**Time:** 4 min x 6          **Pitch size:** 40m x 30m

**The Game:**
- Play 6 v 6
- Each team starts with a football
- They try to maintain possession of their ball whilst attempting to win their opponents'
- If successful they can score a point by playing both balls against each other
- This is a difficult game and requires good peripheral vision

# Exercise 65

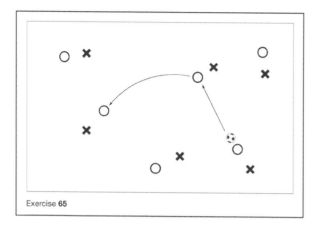

Exercise **65**

**Equipment:** 4 cones, 2 balls        **No of players:** 12

**Time:** 4 min x 6        **Pitch size:** 40m x 30m

**The Game:**
- Play 6 v 6
- Each team tries to maintain possession of the ball
- They score a point if they can chip the ball to a player, who controls the ball on his chest and then successfully passes to a team mate
- If a player controls the ball on his chest but then loses possession or his pass is not successful, then the point is not given
- This is a difficult game and should only be attempted by more experienced players

**Progression**
- Award one point for a chest control and pass, two points for a headed pass and three points for a wall pass
- The pass must reach a team mate

## Exercise 66

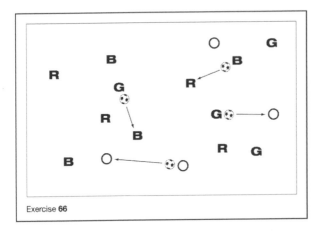

Exercise 66

**Equipment:** 4 cones, 4 sets of bibs, 4 balls  **No of players:** 16

**Time:** 4 min x 6                          **Pitch size:** 30m x 20m

**The Game:**
- The players are divided into four teams, with each team wearing different coloured bibs
- Players randomly pass four balls amongst themselves
- However, they cannot pass to the colour that gave them the ball
- To improve communication, players call out the colour they received from

**Progression**
- When a rhythm has been established, choose one of the colours as the defenders
- This will create a 12 v 4 situation. Start with one ball
- The attackers try to maintain possession, but cannot pass to the colour that gave them the ball
- This should improve concentration as the number of passing lines are reduced
- For more experienced players, introduce a second ball

## Exercise 67

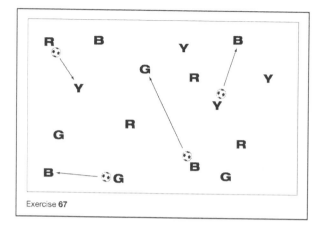

Exercise 67

**Equipment:** 4 cones, 4 sets of bibs, 4 balls     **No of players:** 16

**Time:** 4 min x 6     **Pitch size:** 30m x 20m

### The Game:
- The players are divided into four teams, with each team wearing different coloured bibs
- Players randomly pass four balls amongst themselves
- However, each team is given a rogue colour that it cannot pass to
- For example, red cannot pass to blue, blue cannot pass to yellow, yellow cannot pass to green and green cannot pass to red
- The game should improve field vision

### Progression
- When a rhythm has been established, choose one of the colours as the defenders
- This will create a 12 v 4 situation. Start with one ball
- Greens have been chosen as the defenders
- The attackers try to maintain possession but red cannot pass to blue, blue cannot pass to yellow and yellow cannot pass to red
- This should improve concentration as the number of passing lines are reduced
- For more experienced players, introduce a second ball

## Exercise 68

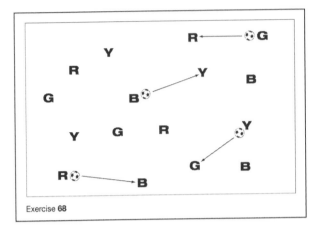

Exercise 68

**Equipment:** 4 cones, 4 sets of bibs, 4 balls   **No of players:** 16

**Time:** 4 min x 6                           **Pitch size:** 30m x 20m

**The Game:**
- The players are divided into four teams, with each team wearing different coloured bibs
- Players randomly pass four balls amongst themselves
- However, they must pass in a predefined sequence e.g. red to blue, blue to yellow, yellow to green and green to red
- The game should improve field vision

**Progression**
- When a rhythm has been established, choose one of the colours as the defenders
- This will create a 12 v 4 situation. Start with one ball
- The defending team are missed out in the sequence e.g. red to blue to green back to red, if yellow are the defenders
- This should improve concentration as the number of passing lines are reduced
- For more experienced players, introduce a second ball

## Exercise 69

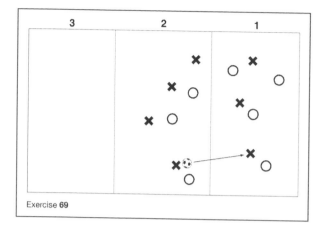

Exercise 69

**Equipment:** 8 cones, set of bibs, balls          **No of players:** 14

**Time:** 3 x 6 min          **Pitch size:** 60m x 40m

**The Game:**

- Play 7 v 7 'keep ball'
- The pitch is divided into three equal zones (40m x 20m), as in the diagram and are numbered 1, 2 and 3
- When the coach calls out a number, the teams compete in that zone
- For example, if he shouts "1 and 2", the teams compete in zones 1 and 2
- If he shouts "3", the players sprint to zone 3 and continue playing
- If he shouts "1" and "3", players will really need to think, as the team will need to split
- The coach should keep changing the zones in order to improve concentration and awareness

## Exercise 70

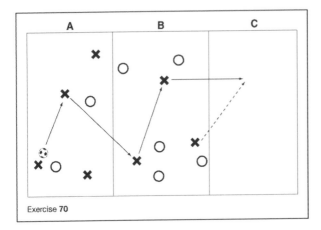

Exercise 70

**Equipment:** 8 cones, set of bibs, balls    **No of players:** 14

**Time:** 3 x 6 min    **Pitch size:** 60m x 25 m

**The Game:**
- Play 7 v 7 keep ball
- The pitch is divided into three equal zones (25m x 20m), as in the dia-gram and are labeled A, B and C. A and C are the outside zones and B the middle zone
- The two teams start by playing in zones A and B. C is the free zone
- The team in possession tries to keep the ball and pass it to a team mate in zone C
- That player CANNOT enter the free zone ahead of the ball
- If the defending team wins the ball, they attempt to do the same thing
- A point is scored if a team can work the ball from one free zone to the other and back

# Exercise 71

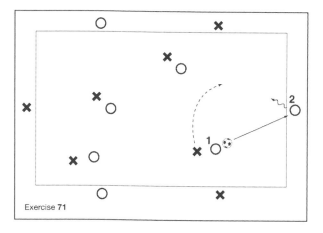

Exercise 71

**Equipment:** 4 cones, set of bibs, balls

**No of players:** 14

**Time:** 3 x 6 min

**Pitch size:** 30m x 20m

**The Game:**

- Four players from each team play inside the grid. Each player is assigned an opponent
- The other three players from each team are placed alternately around the outside of the grid
- The team in possession tries to keep the ball, with the help of the three outside players
- The four inside players from the defending team try to recover the ball
- The team in possession has to make three consecutive passes before they can play to an outside player
- The outside player who receives the ball dribbles into the grid
- The player who passed to him takes his place on the outside
- The defending player who was marking O1 now has to quickly readjust and pick up O2
- This is a very fluid game and players on the outside must always be alive to the changing situation

## Exercise 72

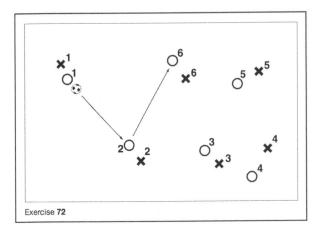

Exercise **72**

**Equipment:** 4 cones, set of bibs, balls   **No of players:** 12

**Time:** 3 x 6 min                                     **Pitch size:** 40m x 30m

**The Game:**
- Play 6 v 6 keep ball
- Players mark 'man to man'. Every player is assigned an opponent from the opposing team
- Each pair can only defend against each other
- Play for three min then let the opposing team start with the ball
- A point is awarded for six consecutive passes

**Progression**
- Play 'man to man' marking, but in the 1 v 1 situation players will not be marking the player who is marking them
- For example, when O1 has the ball, he will be marked by X1, O2 by X2, O3 by X3 and so on
- However, when X's win the ball X1 could be marked by O6, X2 by O5, X3 by O2, X4 by O1, X5 by O3 and X6 by O4
- Who marks who will be decided by the coach at the start of the game
- This is a fast moving game and defenders must be alert at each turn-over

## Exercise 73

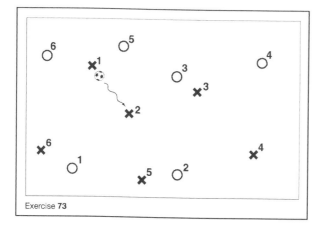

Exercise **73**

**Equipment:** 4 cones, set of bibs, balls       **No of players:** 12

**Time:** 3 x 6 min       **Pitch size:** 40m x 30m

**The Game:**
- Play 6 v 6 'keep ball'
- Each player is given a number from 1 to 6
- The team in possession gets one point every time a player successfully performs a 'take over' with the next number in the sequence
- For example, if X1 completes a 'take over' with X2, then X's score a point
- The coach should allow both teams to practise the sequence before the game becomes competitive

**Progression**
- Play 'man to man' marking
- X1 marks O1, X2 marks O2 and so on
- Teams score a point for every successful 'take over' with the next player in the sequence
- This is a difficult game and should only be attempted by more experienced players

## Exercise 74

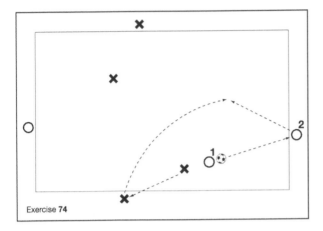

Exercise **74**

**Equipment:** 4 cones, 4 bibs, balls    **No of players:** 8

**Time:** 4-8 x 3 min    **Pitch size:** 20m x 10m

**The Game:**
- Two players from each team play inside the grid. Each player is assigned an opponent
- The other four players are placed alternately on each side of the grid
- The team in possession tries to keep the ball with the help of the two outside players
- The two inside players from the defending team try to recover the ball
- The team in possession has to make two consecutive passes before they can pass to an outside player
- The outside player who receives the ball dribbles into the grid
- The player who passed to him takes his place
- The defending player, who was marking O1, quickly changes places with a team mate on the outside
- The new defender has to find O2 quickly
- This is a very fluid game and players on the outside must always be alive to the changing situation

## Exercise 75

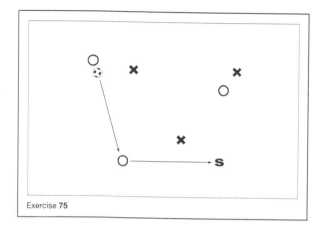

Exercise **75**

**Equipment:** 4 cones, set of bibs, balls          **No of players:** 7

**Time:** 6 x 3 min          **Pitch size:** 25m x 20m

**The Game:**
- Play 3 v 3 plus one support player
- The support player is limited to two touches and plays with the team in possession
- The attacking team tries to keep possession
- If the defenders intercept the ball, then they try to keep it
- Defenders can only intercept the ball, they cannot tackle
- Change the support player every three min
- The coach should have a supply of balls available

**Progression**
- Allow tackling as well as interceptions
- Play man to man marking
- Add a second support player but limit both to one touch

## Exercise 76

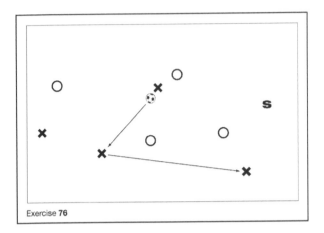

Exercise **76**

**Equipment:** 4 cones, set of bibs, balls     **No of players:** 9

**Time:** 6 x 4 min     **Pitch size:** 40m x 20m

**The Game:**
- Play 4 v 4 plus one support player
- The support player is limited to two touches and plays with the team in possession
- The attacking team tries to maintain possession
- If the defenders intercept the ball then they try to keep it
- Defenders can only intercept the ball, they cannot tackle
- Change the support player every four minutes
- The coach should have a supply of balls available

**Progression**
- Allow tackling as well as interceptions
- Play man to man marking
- Add a second support player but limit both to one touch

# Exercise 77

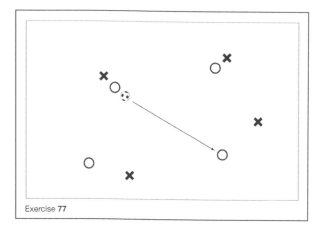

Exercise **77**

**Equipment:** 4 cones, set of bibs, balls          **No of players:** 8

**Time:** 6 x 4 min          **Pitch size:** 40m x 20m

## The Game:

- Play 4 v 4
- Two players from each team mark man to man
- The other four players are free to mark anybody
- The attacking team tries to keep possession
- If the defenders win the ball, then they try to keep it
- The coach should have a supply of balls available
- Change the man to man marking players every four minutes

## Exercise 78

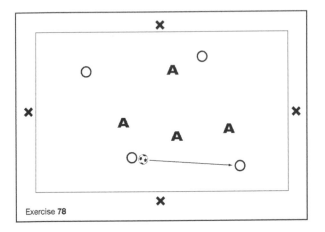

Exercise **78**

**Equipment:** 4 cones, 2 sets of bibs, balls     **No of players:** 12

**Time:** 6-10 x 3 min                              **Pitch size:** 30m x 25m

**The Game:**
- Play 4 v 4 plus 4. Two teams of four players try to maintain possession of the ball
- The attacking team may use the outside players for support
- The outside players only have two touches and cannot be tackled

**Progression 1**
The team that completes six consecutive passes remains on the field and the losing team takes the place of those on the outside

**Progression 2**
The team that completes six consecutive passes takes the place of those on the outside

**Progression 3**
- The team that completes six consecutive passes remains on the field and the losing team takes the place of those on the outside
- However, the game is continuous and the winning team carry on playing, in an attempt to complete six more passes
- The outside team must react to the situation and move onto the pitch at speed in order to prevent this
- This is a fast moving game and players must focus, particularly when waiting to enter the grid

# Exercise 79

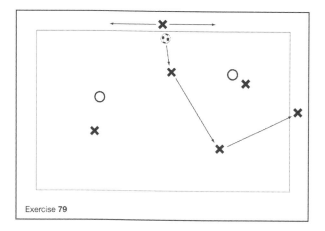

Exercise **79**

**Equipment:** 4 cones, set of bibs, balls       **No of players:** 8

**Time:** 6-10 x 3 min       **Pitch size:** 15m x 10m

## The Game:
- Play 6 v 2
- Six attackers, with two on the outside and four in the middle, try to maintain possession against two defenders
- The outside players are limited to two touches and cannot be tackled
- They are allowed to move around the outside of the grid, but must always be on different sides
- The defenders should be changed every three min, as this exercise is very demanding

## Progression
- The two support players stand just inside the grid
- This will make the space much tighter

## Exercise 80

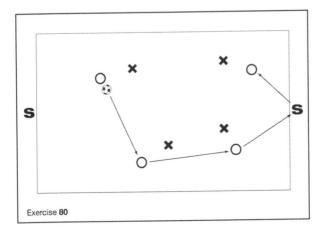

Exercise 80

**Equipment:** 4 cones, set of bibs, balls    **No of players:** 10

**Time:** 4-8 x 4 min    **Pitch size:** 25m x 20m

### The Game:
- Play 4 v 4 plus 2. Four attackers try to work the ball from one end player to the other and back
- If successful, they earn a point
- The end players return the ball to the team that passed to them
- Change the end players every four minutes

## Exercise 81

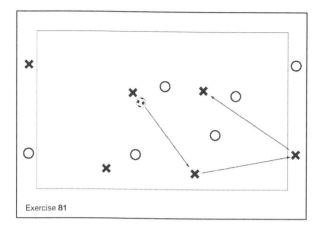

Exercise 81

**Equipment:** 4 cones, set of bibs, balls     **No of players:** 12

**Time:** 4-8 x 4 min     **Pitch size:** 25m x 20m

**The Game:**
- Play 4 v 4 plus 2 plus 2. Four attackers try to work the ball from their own end player and back
- If successful, they earn a point
- The outside players cannot be tackled and are limited to two touches

**Progression**
Whoever passes to the end player takes his place

## Exercise 82

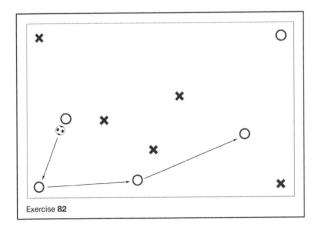

Exercise **82**

**Equipment:** 4 cones, set of bibs, balls          **No of players:** 10

**Time:** 6-10 x 3 min          **Pitch size:** 25m square

**The Game:**
- Play 3 v 3 plus 2. Two players from each team stand at diagonally opposite corners of the square, with two teams of three in the square
- The attacking team tries to keep possession of the ball and work it from one corner player to the other and back
- If successful, they earn a point
- Change the corner players every three min

**Progression**
- Teams score a point for eight consecutive passes
- Whoever passes to the corner player takes his place

# Exercise 83

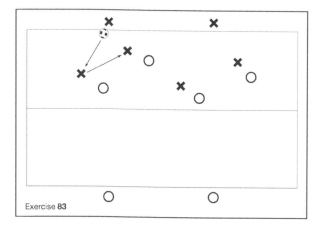

Exercise **83**

**Equipment:** 6 cones, set of bibs, balls     **No of players:** 12

**Time:** 4-8 x 5 min     **Pitch size:** 50m x 20m

## The Game:

- Play 6 v 6. The field is divided into two zones (25m by 20m), with two players from each team standing on opposite end lines
- Both teams try to maintain possession of the ball in their end zone, where they have an advantage of a 6 v 4 situation
- If the defending team wins the ball, they transfer it to one of their end players as quickly as possible and then try to maintain possession in their own zone
- Each team gains a point for six consecutive passes

## Exercise 84

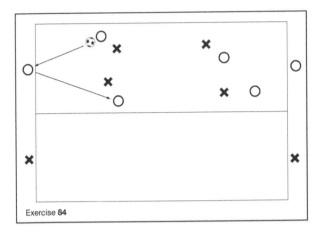

Exercise **84**

**Equipment:** 6 cones, set of bibs, balls     **No of players:** 12

**Time:** 4-8 x 5 min     **Pitch size:** 50m x 20m

**The Game:**
- Play 6 v 6. The field is divided into two zones (25m by 20m), with two players from each team standing on the sidelines of their attacking zone
- Both teams try to maintain possession of the ball in their zone
- Here they have the advantage of a 6 v 4 situation
- If the defending team wins the ball, they attempt to transfer it to one of their side players, as quickly as possible and then maintain possession
- Each team gains a point for six consecutive passes in their attacking zone

## Exercise 85

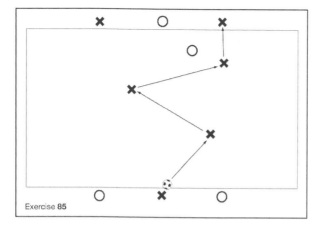

Exercise **85**

**Equipment:** 4 cones, set of bibs, balls

**No of players:** 12

**Time:** 8-10 x 3 min

**Pitch size:** 30m x 25m

### The Game:
- Play 6 v 6. The teams play 3 v 3 in the middle, with a further three players from each team placed on either end line, as shown in the diagram
- The attacking team tries to maintain possession of the ball and work it from one end player to another and back
- If successful, they earn a point
- The end players are limited to two touches

### Progression
- The player who passes to the end player takes his place
- There must be a minimum of two passes before the ball can be transferred to an end player

## Exercise 86

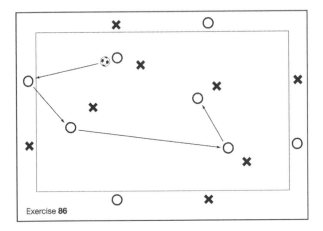

Exercise **86**

**Equipment:** 4 cones, set of bibs, balls        **No of players:** 16

**Time:** 8 x 4 min        **Pitch size:** 35m x 25m

**The Game:**
- Play 8 v 8. Each team has four players on the outside of the pitch and four in the middle
- The attacking team tries to maintain possession of the ball, with the help of its outside players
- The outside players (who cannot be tackled) may only pass to an inside player, not to another outside player
- However, the outside players cannot pass back to the player who gave them the ball

**Progression 1**
The ball has to be passed in sequence i.e. from an outside player, to an inside player, to an outside player and so on

**Progression 2**
- The outside players are limited to one touch
- If they take more than one touch, then they must pass to another outside player
- That player returns the ball to the grid

# Exercise 87

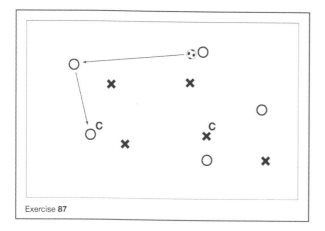

Exercise **87**

**Equipment:** 4 cones, set of bibs, balls    **No of players:** 10

**Time:** 4-8 x 4 min    **Pitch size:** 40m x 30m

## The Game:

- Play 5 v 5. Each team nominates a 'Captain'
- The attacking team tries to maintain possession of the ball
- Every time the 'Captain' receives the ball and follows with a successful pass, then their team wins a point

## Progression

- After five consecutive passes, the team gains a point if the sixth pass reaches the 'Captain'
- To make this game easier, the 'Captains' could be goalkeepers, who have the use of hands as well as feet

# Exercise 88

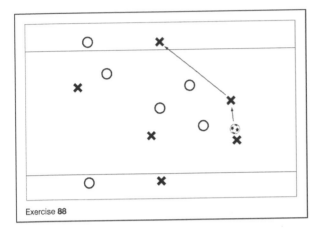

Exercise 88

**Equipment:** 8 cones, set of bibs, balls    **No of players:** 12

**Time:** 4-8 x 4 min    **Pitch size:** 40m x 30m

**The Game:**
- Play 6 v 6. Each team has two players in the outside zones (30m by 5m) and four in the central zone (30m by 30m)
- The attacking team tries to maintain possession of the ball, with the help of their outside players
- The outside players cannot tackle each other

**Progression 1**
- The outside players compete against each other
- The person who passes to the outside player takes his place, whilst the outside player must dribble into the central zone at pace, before passing the ball
- It is essential that a high intensity is maintained

**Progression 2**
- Players mark 'man to man' and can only tackle their own player
- The attacking team attempt to slip their marker in order to maintain possession of the ball

## Exercise 89

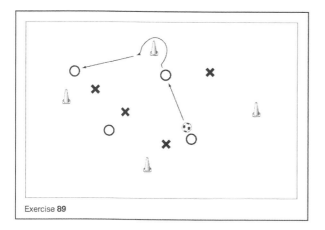

Exercise **89**

**Equipment:** 8 cones, bibs, balls    **No of players:** 8

**Time:** 6 x 4 min    **Pitch size:** 40m square

**The Game:**
- Play 4 v 4
- Each team attacks and defends four cones that are placed inside the square, as in the diagram
- Players score a point if they can dribble around a cone and then pass to a team mate
- If they dribble around a cone but don't successfully pass to a team mate, then the point is not given

**Progression**
- Each team attacks and defends two cones that are placed on opposite sides of the square
- Players score a point if they can dribble around one of the cones they are attacking and then pass to a team mate
- If they dribble around a cone but don't successfully pass to a team mate, then the point is not given

**Chapter 11**

# Attacking a Line, Shape or Zone

## Exercise 90

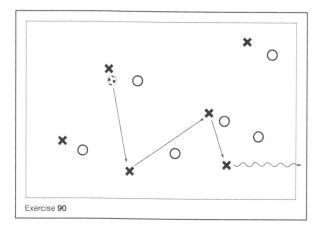

Exercise **90**

**Equipment:** 4 cones, set of bibs, balls    **No of players:** 12

**Time:** 4-8 x 6 min with 2 min recovery    **Pitch size:** 50m x 30m

**The Game:**
- Play 6 v 6. Each team attacks and defends a line
- The attacking team scores a point if it dribbles the ball, under control, over the opponents' end line

**Progression**
After scoring, the team maintains possession and attacks in the opposite direction

## Exercise 91

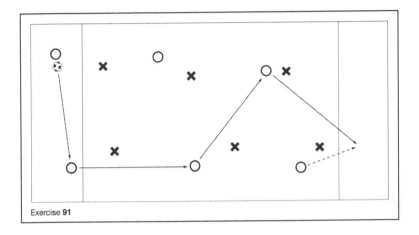

Exercise 91

**Equipment:** 8 cones, set of bibs, balls          **No of players:** 12

**Time:** 4-8 x 6 min with 2 min recovery          **Pitch size:** 50m x 30m

**The Game:**
- Play 6 v 6. Each team attacks and defends a marked zone (5m by 30m)
- The attacking team attempts to pass the ball to a team mate, who receives it in the end zone
- The receiving player cannot wait in the end zone, but has to move into it as the ball is played

**Progression** 1
To encourage playing out from the back, the attacking team may use its own defensive zone to maintain possession. Here, they cannot be challenged by the opposition

**Progression** 2
- To score, the receiving player has to control the ball in the attacking zone (as above) and then dribble over the end line
- A defender can attempt to win the ball at any time

## Exercise 92

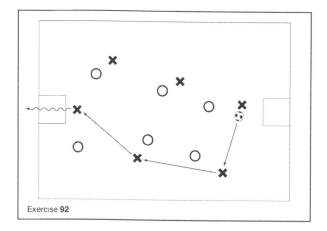

Exercise **92**

**Equipment:** 16 cones, set of bibs, balls    **No of players:** 12

**Time:** 2-6 x 8 min with 2 min recovery    **Pitch size:** 40m x 35m

### The Game:
- Play 6 v 6
- Each team attacks and defends two squares (6m by 6m)
- The attacking team attempts to score by entering the front of a square and dribbling the ball over the end line
- Teams may ONLY attack from the front of the square (as in the diagram)
- Players in possession can be tackled at any time

## Exercise 93

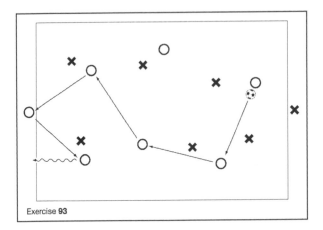

Exercise **93**

**Equipment:** 4 cones, set of bibs, balls        **No of players:** 14

**Time:** 3-6 x 8 min with 2 min recovery        **Pitch size:** 50m x 30m

**The Game:**
- Play 7 v 7
- A player from each team stands on opposite end lines, as in the diagram
- The attacking team tries to maintain possession and pass to their end player
- The end player has to pass back first time to any of his team
- This player then attempts to dribble over the end line to score
- The scorer changes places with the end player

# Exercise 94

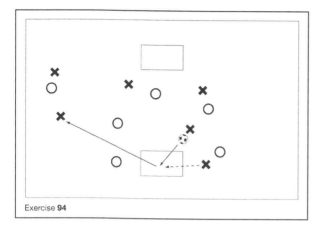

Exercise **94**

**Equipment:** 12 cones, set of bibs, balls   **No of players:** 12

**Time:** 4-8 x 8 min with 2 min recovery   **Pitch size:** 50m square

## The Game:
- Play 6 v 6
- Two five-metre squares are marked out inside the large square
- Each team has one square to attack and one to defend
- One of the players from the attacking team must run into his square, at the right time, to receive a pass
- If the ball is not controlled, the goal does not count
- If the ball is controlled in the square but not successfully passed to a team mate, then the goal does not count
- Defenders are not allowed into their defensive square

## Exercise 95

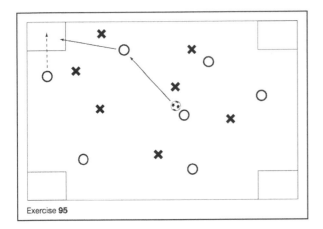

Exercise **95**

**Equipment:** 16 cones, set of bibs, balls    **No of players:** 14

**Time:** 4-6 x 10 min with 2 min recovery    **Pitch size:** 50m square

**The Game:**
- Play 7 v 7. Four five-metre squares are marked out in each corner of the large square
- The team in possession can attack any of the four smaller squares
- To score, one of the players from the attacking team must run into a square, at the right time, to receive a pass
- Defenders are not allowed into the square

**Progression 1**
After receiving the ball in the square, the attacker has to successfully pass to a team mate for the goal to count

**Progression 2**
Teams attack two squares and defend two squares

**Progression 3**
Teams attack two diagonal squares and defend two diagonal squares

## Exercise 96

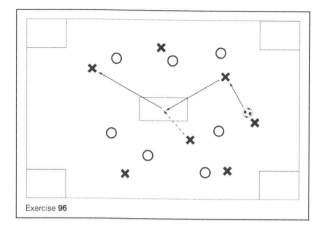

Exercise **96**

**Equipment:** 20 cones, set of bibs, balls     **No of players:** 14

**Time:** 4-6 x 8 min with 2 min recovery     **Pitch size:** 50m square

### The Game:
- Play 7 v 7
- Four five-metre squares are marked out in the corners of the large square, and a fifth in the centre of the square
- The team in possession can attack any of the five small squares
- To score, one of the players from the attacking team must run into a square, at the right time, to receive a pass
- After controlling the ball, he must then successfully pass to a team mate
- Defenders are not allowed into the square

### Progression
- Teams attack two squares and defend two
- The middle square can be used by either team

## Exercise 97

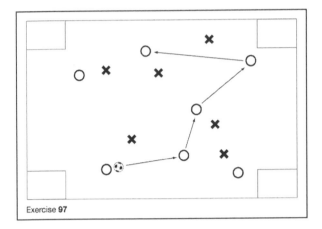

Exercise 97

**Equipment:** 16 cones, set of bibs, balls    **No of players:** 13

**Time:** 4-8 x 6 min with 1 min recovery    **Pitch size:** 50m square

**The Game:**
- Play 6 v 7
- Four five-metre squares are marked out
- The team with superior numbers tries to maintain possession of the ball
- The team with inferior numbers tries to maintain possession of the ball and then one of its players runs into a corner square, at the right time, to receive a pass
- Defenders are not allowed into the square
- Change the teams every five minutes

# Exercise 98

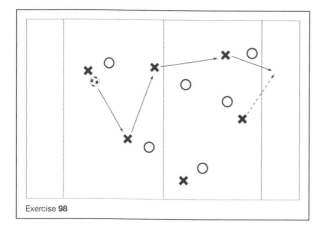

Exercise **98**

**Equipment:** 10 cones, set of bibs, balls    **No of players:** 12

**Time:** 4-8 x 6 min with 2 min recovery    **Pitch size:** 50m x 35m

## The Game:
- Play 6 v 6
- Each team attacks and defends a marked zone (5m by 35m)
- The attacking team may ONLY have three touches of the ball in its own half, but as many as it likes in the attacking half
- This should improve "game speed"
- To score, one of the players from the attacking team should run into the opponents' zone to receive the ball
- The score does not count if the ball is not controlled

## Exercise 99

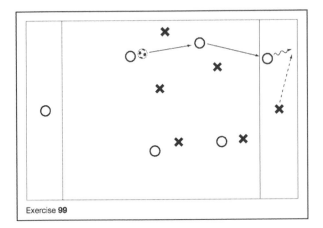

Exercise **99**

**Equipment:** 8 cones, set of bibs, balls        **No of players:** 12

**Time:** 4-8 x 6 min with 2 min recovery        **Pitch size:** 50m x 30m

**The Game:**
- Play 6 v 6
- Each team attacks and defends a zone (5m by 30m) in which a defender is situated
- The attacking team tries to maintain possession of the ball and make a final pass into the end zone, for a player to control and dribble over the end line
- The defender has to read the situation and try to stop the attacker from receiving the ball in the end zone or prevent him from dribbling over the end line
- Change the defender every time a goal is scored

## Exercise 100

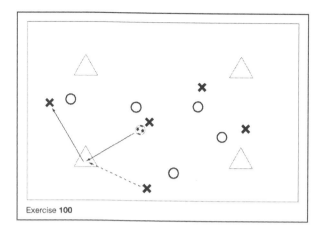

Exercise **100**

**Equipment:** 16 cones, set of bibs, balls    **No of players:** 10

**Time:** 4-8 x 4 min with 2 min recovery    **Pitch size:** 40m x 35m

**The Game:**
- Play 5 v 5
- The attacking team tries to maintain possession of the ball and pass to a player who has moved into one of the four triangles (4m)
- A point is scored if the ball is received under control and passed out to a teammate.
- The team in possession then tries to attack one of the other three triangles
- Defenders cannot enter a triangle

**Progression** 1
Teams attack and defend two triangles

**Progression** 2
Teams attack and defend two diagonal triangles

## Exercise 101

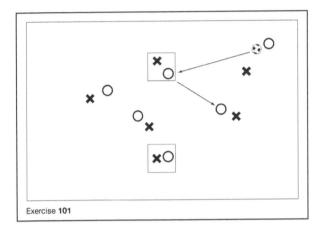

Exercise **101**

**Equipment:** 12 cones, set of bibs, balls     **No of players:** 12

**Time:** 4-8 x 4 min with 1 min recovery     **Pitch size:** 40m square

**The Game:**
- Play 6 v 6
- Two eight-metre squares are set up and a player from each side is placed in each one
- The attacking team tries to maintain possession of the ball and pass to a teammate in one of the squares
- The defender in the square tries to prevent this
- If the ball is passed into the square and out again to a team mate, one point is scored
- The ball cannot be passed back to the player who played the ball into the square
- Change the players in the squares every four minutes

# Exercise 102

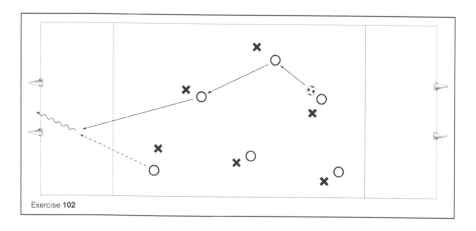

Exercise **102**

**Equipment:** 12 cones, set of bibs, balls    **No of players:** 12

**Time:** 4-8 x 6 min with 2 min recovery    **Pitch size:** 50m x 30m

## The Game:
- Play 6 v 6
- Each team attacks and defends a large goal (12m)
- The attacking team tries to maintain possession of the ball and pass to a player who has moved into the attacking zone (10m by 30m)
- This player has to control the ball and then attempt to dribble through the goal
- Neither the defender nor the attacker can wait in the zone
- Players only move in as the ball is played

## Exercise 103

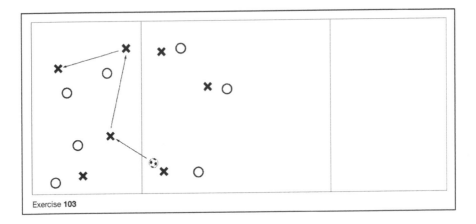

Exercise **103**

**Equipment:** 8 cones, set of bibs, balls       **No of players:** 14

**Time:** 4-8 x 6 min with 2 min recovery       **Pitch size:** 50m x 40m

### The Game:
- Play 7 v 7
- Each team attacks and defends a zone (15m by 40m)
- The attacking team tries to maintain possession of the ball and progress into the opponents' end zone
- Here they score a point for five consecutive passes
- The attacking team has to leave some players in the middle zone in case their opponents win the ball and break out quickly

# Exercise 104

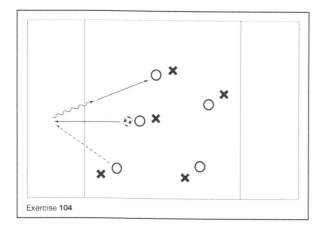

Exercise **104**

**Equipment:** 16 cones, set of bibs, balls    **No of players:** 10

**Time:** 4-8 x 5 min with 2 min recovery    **Pitch size:** 40m x 35m

**The Game:**
- Play 5 v 5
- The attacking team tries to keep possession of the ball and pass to a player who has moved into one of the marked zones (5m x 5m)
- The team scores a point if the player receives the ball under control, dribbles out of the zone and successfully passes to a team mate

**Progression**
Players mark man to man

## Exercise 105

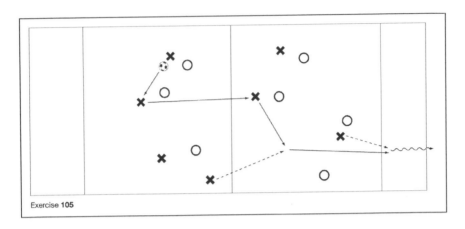

Exercise 105

**Equipment:** 10 cones, set of bibs, balls     **No of players:** 14

**Time:** 4-8 x 8 min with 2 min recovery     **Pitch size:** 50m x 40m

**The Game:**
- Play 7 v 7. Each team attacks and defends a zone (5m by 40m)
- The field is divided into two, with four defenders and three attackers in each half
- The attacking team tries to progress into its opponents' half. If successful, they can be joined by one of their four defenders
- Here they try to pass to a player who has moved into the attacking zone
- They score a point if this player controls the ball and dribbles over the end line
- They then have to re-form quickly i.e. four defenders and three attackers

## Exercise 106

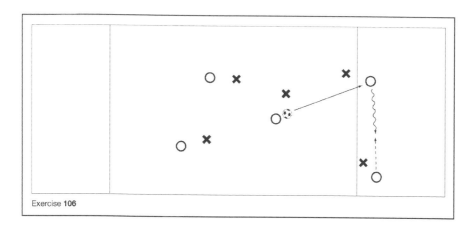

Exercise **106**

**Equipment:** 8 cones, set of bibs, balls   **No of players:** 10

**Time:** 4 – 8 x 5 min   **Pitch size:** 40m x 30m

### The Game:
Play 5 v 5
- Each team attacks and defends a marked zone (5m x 30m)
- The team in possession of the ball scores one point if they can perform a 'take over' in their opponents' defensive zone

### Progression
If a team manages to perform a take over in their opponents' zone, they maintain possession and attack in the opposite direction

## Exercise 107

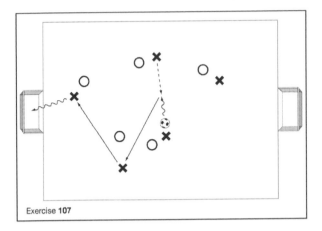

Exercise 107

**Equipment:** 8 cones, set of bibs, balls    **No of players:** 10

**Time:** 4-8 x 5 min    **Pitch size:** 40m x 30m

**The Game:**
- Play 5 v 5
- Each team attacks and defends a 10m goal
- Teams score by dribbling through the goal they are attacking, with the ball under control
- However, before they can score, the attacking team must perform a take over in the build up

## Exercise 108

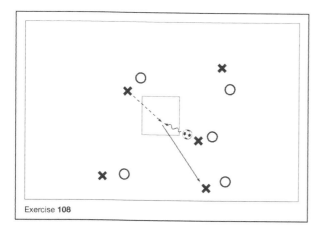

Exercise **108**

**Equipment:** 8 cones, set of bibs, balls

**No of players:** 10

**Time:** 4-8 x 5 min

**Pitch size:** 40m x 30m

### The Game:

- Play 5 v 5
- A five-metre square is marked out in the middle of the pitch
- The team in possession scores one point if two players manage to perform a take over in the five-metre square
- They score an extra point if two players perform a take over in the five-metre square and then successfully pass to a team mate

## Exercise 109

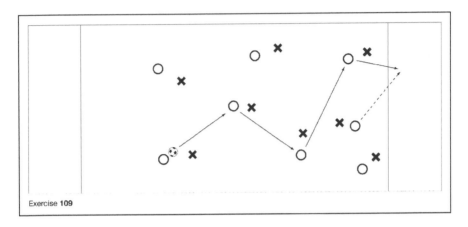

Exercise **109**

**Equipment:** 8 cones, set of bibs, balls          **No of players:** 16

**Time:** 4 x 8 min          **Pitch size:** 40m x 30m

**The Game:**
- Play 8 v 8
- Each team attacks and defends a five-metre zone
- Players pass by hand and can only hold the ball for three seconds
- Defenders can only intercept the ball, they cannot snatch it out of a player's hands
- Attackers score by completing a pass to a team mate in the end zone
- After scoring, attackers keep possession and attack in the other direction

**Progression 1**
- The player receiving the ball in the end zone has to control the ball first with any part of his body, before catching it
- He gets an extra point if he controls the ball without using his hands and then juggles it three times

**Progression 2**
- The receiver in the end zone controls the ball, then volleys it back to a team mate or heads the ball back directly to a team mate on the field
- The team now attacks in the opposite direction

## Exercise 110

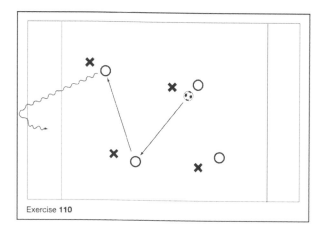

Exercise **110**

**Equipment:** 8 cones, set of bibs, balls    **No of players:** 8

**Time:** 4-8 x 5 min    **Pitch size:** 35m x 25m

### The Game:
- Play 4 v 4
- Each team attacks and defends a five-metre zone
- A player scores by dribbling the ball across the opponent's end line, then playing the ball back with an inside or outside cut, before controlling it in the end zone
- A defender can enter the end zone and challenge the player with the ball at any time
- The coach should keep changing the turn required on the end line

Chapter 12

# Attacking a Target

## Exercise 111

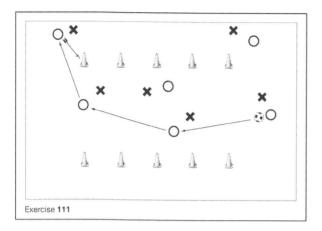

Exercise **111**

**Equipment:** 14 cones, set of bibs, balls    **No of players:** 12

**Time:** 5-8 x 5 min with 2 min recovery    **Pitch size:** 50m x 40m

**The Game:**
- Play 6 v 6
- Each team attacks and defends a row of cones (five or more). The cones are placed one metre apart, in a straight line
- The attacking team tries to maintain possession of the ball and knock over the opponents' cone
- Play is allowed in front of and behind the line of cones

**Progression 1**
Cones can only be knocked down by a one-touch finish

**Progression 2**
Each team has a goalkeeper, who defends the cones

**Progression 3**
- The cones are positioned anywhere in the team's own half of the field
- To increase the intensity, add another ball

## Exercise 112

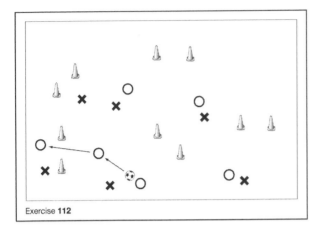

Exercise **112**

**Equipment:** 12 cones or poles, set of bibs, balls    **No of players:** 12

**Time:** 4-8 x 5 min with 1 minute recovery    **Pitch size:** 50m x 40m

### The Game:
- Play 6 v 6
- Set up several goals (2m wide) on the field
- Attackers score by completing a pass to a team mate through a goal
- Teams cannot score twice in a row in the same goal

### Progression 1
Attackers score by dribbling through a small goal and then successfully passing to a team mate

### Progression 2
- One team scores by completing a pass to a team mate through a goal whilst the other team scores a point for eight consecutive passes.
- Change roles every five minutes

## Exercise 113

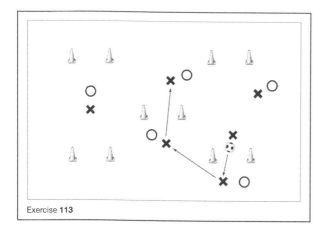

Exercise **113**

**Equipment:** 14 cones, set of bibs, balls    **No of players:** 12

**Time:** 4-8 x 6 min with 2 min recovery    **Pitch size:** 50m x 35m

**The Game:**
*   Play 6 v 6
*   Each team attacks and defends two goals (3m) and a common goal in the middle of the pitch
*   The attacking team tries to maintain possession of the ball and goals are scored by playing the ball through a goal to a team mate
*   Goals can be scored from either side of the cones

**Progression**
Attackers score by dribbling through a goal and then successfully passing to a team mate

## Exercise 114

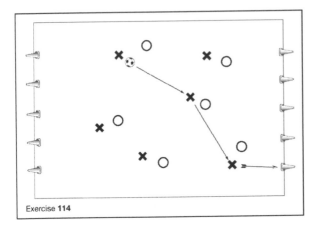

Exercise **114**

**Equipment:** 14 cones, set of bibs, balls   **No of players:** 12

**Time:** 4-8 x 5 min with 2 min recovery   **Pitch size:** 50m x 30m

### The Game:
- Play 6 v 6. Each team attacks and defends five cones placed on the end lines of the pitch
- After five consecutive passes, the attacking team tries to knock over one of their opponents' cones
- A point is scored for every cone hit

### Progression 1
If successful, the team attacks in the opposite direction

### Progression 2
Teams can attack immediately without making five consecutive passes

### Progression 3
The cones are defended by a goalkeeper

# Exercise 115

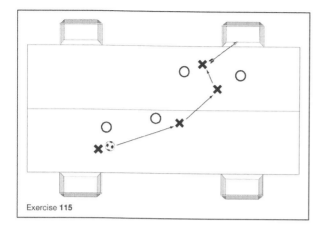

Exercise **115**

**Equipment:** 8 cones or poles, set of bibs, balls   **No of players:** 8

**Time:** 4-8 x 4 min with 2 min recovery   **Pitch size:** 30m x 25m

## The Game:
- Play 4 v 4
- Each team attacks and defends two small goals (3m)
- The attacking team tries to keep possession and score through one of the opponents' goals

## Progression 1
An attacking player scores by dribbling through one of his opponents' goals

## Progression 2
Two players are restricted to their own half and two to their opponents' half

## Exercise 116

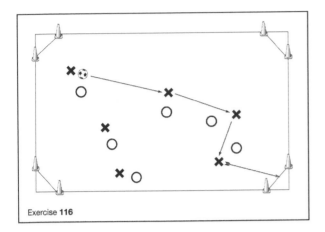

Exercise **116**

**Equipment:** 12 cones, set of bibs, balls

**No of players:** 12

**Time:** 4-8 x 5 min with 2 min recovery

**Pitch size:** 50m x 30m

### The Game:
- Play 6 v 6
- Each team attacks and defends two small goals (3m) placed across the corners of the pitch
- The attacking team tries to maintain possession and pass the ball through one of their opponents' goals

### Progression
- An attacking player has to dribble through one of his opponents' goals, with the ball under control
- If successful, the team attacks in the opposite direction

## Exercise 117

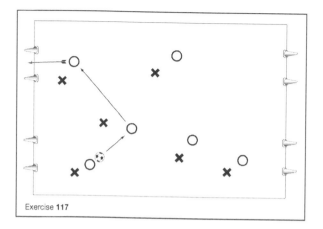

Exercise **117**

**Equipment:** 8 cones or poles, set of bibs, balls    **No of players:** 12

**Time:** 4-8 x 5 min with 2 min recovery    **Pitch size:** 50m x 30m

**The Game:**
- Play 6 v 6
- Each team attacks and defends two small goals (2m) situated on the sides of the pitch
- The attacking team tries to maintain possession and score through one of the two opponents' goals

**Progression 1**
Score with a one-touch finish

**Progression 2**
An attacking player scores by dribbling through one of the opponents' goals

## Exercise 118

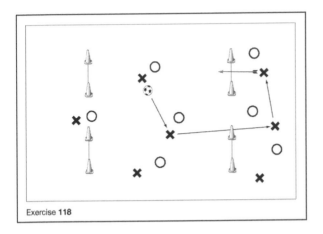

Exercise **118**

**Equipment:** 8 cones or poles, set of bibs, balls   **No of players:** 14

**Time:** 4-8 x 6 min

**Pitch size:** 50m x 30m

### The Game:
- Play 7 v 7
- Each team attacks and defends two lateral goals (3m)
- The attacking team tries to maintain possession of the ball and score through one of the opponents' goals

### Progression 1
The ball has to be passed through one of the opponents' goals to a team mate

### Progression 2
An attacking player dribbles through one of the opponents' goals and then passes to a team mate

### Progression 3
Attackers perform a take over in either of the opponents' goals

## Exercise 119

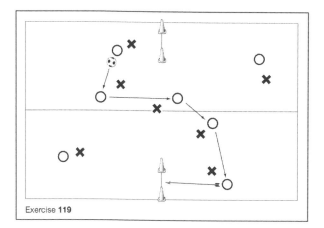

Exercise 119

**Equipment:** 4 cones or poles, set of bibs, balls      **No of players:** 14

**Time:** 4-6 x 6min with 2 min recovery      **Pitch size:** 50m x 30m

### The Game:
- Play 7v 7
- Each team attacks and defends a lateral goal (3m)
- The team in possession is limited to two touches in its own half, but is allowed free play in the attacking half
- A shot can be taken from either side of the goal

### Progression 1
Free play is allowed in both halves of the pitch

### Progression 2
The lateral goals are widened (6m) and a goalkeeper is placed in each

## Exercise 120

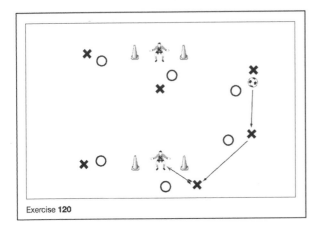

Exercise **120**

**Equipment:** 4 cones, 4 poles, set of bibs, balls   **No of players:** 14

**Time:** 4-6 x 6 min with 2 min recovery        **Pitch size:** 50m x 35m

### The Game:
- Play 7 v 7
- Each team attacks and defends a goal (6m)
- Both goals are 10m in from the end line
- The attacking team can shoot from either side of the goal
- If a goal is scored and they retain possession, the attacking team can immediately shoot again
- This will ensure that the defenders and goalkeeper react quickly

### Progression
Players mark man to man

# Exercise 121

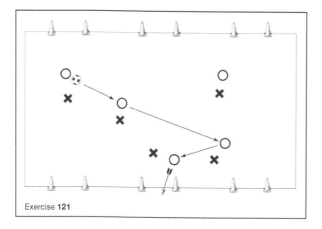

Exercise **121**

**Equipment:** 16 cones, set of bibs, balls          **No of players:** 10

**Time:** 4-6 x 5 min          **Pitch size:** 50m x 30m

**The Game:**
*   Play 5 v 5
*   Each team attacks and defends three small goals (2m), as shown in the diagram
*   The attacking team tries to maintain possession and score in any of the opponents' goals

**Progression 1**
Players mark man to man

**Progression 2**
Teams score by dribbling through one of their opponents' goals. If successful, they keep possession and attack in the opposite direction

**Progression 3**
One team is limited to two touches

## .Exercise 122

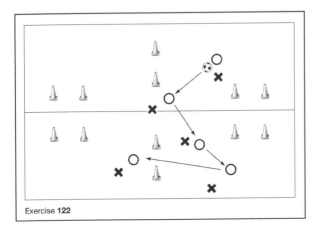

Exercise **122**

**Equipment:** 16 cones, set of bibs, balls

**No of players:** 10

**Time:** 4-8 x 5 min

**Pitch size:** 50m x 30m

**The Game:**
- Play 5 v 5
- Each team attacks and defends three small goals (2m) positioned as in the diagram
- The attacking team tries to maintain possession and then pass through an opponent's goal, to a team mate
- Teams cannot score in the same goal twice in a row

**Progression 1**
An attacking player scores by dribbling through an opponent's goal and then successfully passes to a team mate

**Progression 2**
Score with a one-touch finish

**Progression 3**
Teams score by performing a take over in any of the opponents' goals

## Exercise 123

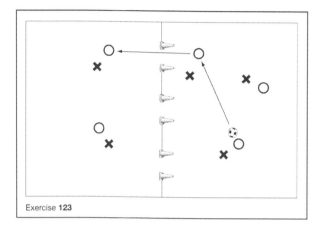

Exercise 123

**Equipment:** 10 cones, set of bibs, balls    **No of players:** 10

**Time:** 4-8 x 5 min    **Pitch size:** 40m x 30m

### The Game:
- Play 5 v 5
- Three small goals (3m) are placed in the middle of the pitch, as in the diagram
- The attacking team tries to maintain possession of the ball and pass to a team mate through one of the goals
- Teams cannot score in the same goal twice

### Progression 1
Teams score from a one-touch pass through the goal

### Progression 2
Play man to man marking

## Exercise 124

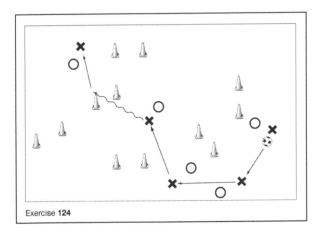

Exercise 124

**Equipment:** 16 cones, set of bibs, balls   **No of players:** 10

**Time:** 4-8 x 5 min   **Pitch size:** 40m x 30m

### The Game:
- Play 5 v 5
- The attacking team tries to maintain possession
- After three consecutive passes, they score a point by dribbling through any of the six small goals (2m) and then passing to a team mate

### Progression 1
Play man to man marking

### Progression 2
Teams score a point by performing a take over in any of the six goals

## Exercise 125

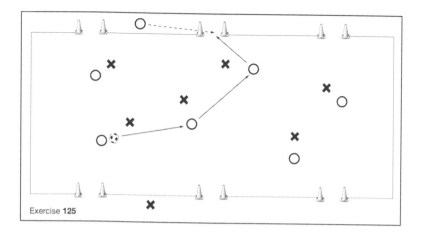

Exercise **125**

**Equipment:** 16 cones, set of bibs, balls          **No of players:** 14

**Time:** 4-6 x 8 min          **Pitch size:** 40m x 35m

### The Game:
*   Play 7 v 7
*   Each team attacks and defends three small goals (3m)
*   One player from each team stands behind the three goals that his team are attacking
*   Every time a pass is made through a goal to the receiving player, a point is scored
*   Players can't score in the same goal twice
*   This game requires great anticipation from the receiving player

### Progression 1
The ball has to be chipped to the receiving player

### Progression 2
The first team to score five goals wins

### Progression 3
The player who scores changes places with the goal minder

## Exercise 126

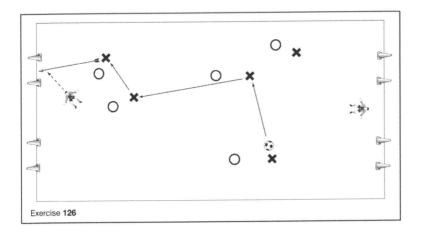

Exercise **126**

**Equipment:** 8 cones, set of bibs, balls          **No of players:** 12

**Time:** 4-8 x 5 min          **Pitch size:** 40m x 30m

**The Game:**
- Play 5 v 5 + 2 goalkeepers
- Each team attacks and defends two small goals (3m) defended by a goalkeeper
- The attacking team tries to maintain possession of the ball, change the direction of play and shoot through one of the opponents' goals.

**Progression 1**
Play two-touch

**Progression 2**
Players score with a one-touch finish

# Exercise 127

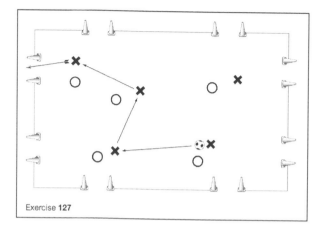

Exercise **127**

**Equipment:** 20 cones, set of bibs, balls    **No of players:** 10

**Time:** 4-8 x 5 min    **Pitch size:** 40m x 30m

## The Game:
- Play 5 v 5
- The attacking team attempts to keep the ball
- After three consecutive passes, the team in possession can score in any of the eight small goals (2m) situated on the sides of the pitch, as in the diagram
- The finish has to be one-touch

## Progression 1
One team attempts to score in the goals whilst the other team scores a point for eight consecutive passes

## Progression 2
Each team attacks and defends four goals

## Exercise 128

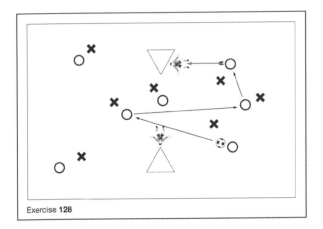

Exercise **128**

**Equipment:** 10 cones, set of bibs, balls

**No of players:** 16

**Time:** 4 x 8 min

**Pitch size:** 50m x 35m

**The Game:**
- Play 7 v 7 + 2 goalkeepers
- Each team attacks and defends a triangular goal (6m)
- The attacking team tries to keep possession and shoot into their opponents' goal
- If successful, they immediately attack in the opposite direction

**Progression**
Play man to man marking

# Exercise 129

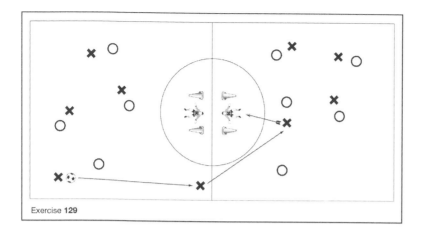

Exercise **129**

**Equipment:** 4 cones, 4 poles, set of bibs, balls   **No of players:** 20

**Time:** 4-6 x 8 min

**Pitch size:** 60m x 50m

## The Game:
- Play 9 v 9 plus two goalkeepers
- There are four open goals in the centre circle, each six metres wide
- Place the goalkeepers in two of the opposite goals, as in the diagram. Each defends one front goal and the goal on their right
- No outfield players are allowed in the centre circle
- One team attempts to score in any of the four goals, whilst the other team tries to win the ball and maintain possession
- Any shots higher than the posts are disallowed
- If the goalkeeper stops a shot, he throws it to the team who is trying to keep possession. He should look for the player furthest away from him
- Play for eight minutes, then change roles

## Progression
- Each goalkeeper plays for a team and has two goals to defend
- Both teams are now trying to score. If the defending team win the ball, they have to complete three consecutive passes before they can shoot
- As before, no outfield player is allowed in the centre circle

## Exercise 130

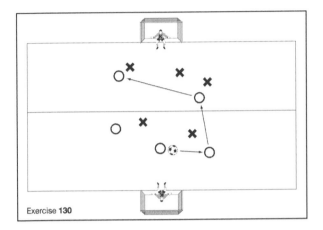

Exercise **130**

**Equipment:** 2 goals, set of bibs, balls

**No of players:** 12

**Time:** 4-8 x 5 min

**Pitch size:** 40m x 30m

### The Game:
- Play 5 v 5 + 2 goalkeepers. Each team attacks and defends a goal protected by a goalkeeper.
- Three players are situated in the defensive zone and two in the attacking zone
- The team in possession tries to pass the ball to one of their players in the attacking zone
- One player from the defensive zone may join in the attack (3 v 3), but must return to the defensive zone when the attack is over

### Progression 1
Two-touch in the defensive zone, free play in the attacking zone

### Progression 2
- A player from the defensive zone cannot join his attackers
- This puts the two attackers in a more realistic game situation

# Exercise 131

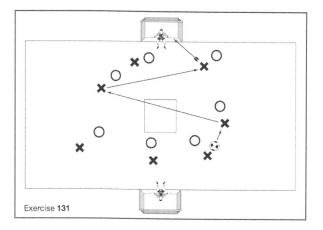

Exercise **131**

**Equipment:** 2 goals, set of bibs, balls, 4 cones   **No of players:** 16

**Time:** 4-8 x 8 min

**Pitch size:** 50m x 40m

## The Game:
- Play 7 v 7 plus two goalkeepers
- A central zone is set up (15m x 15m), as in the diagram
- Each team attacks and defends a goal
- The ball can be played across the central zone but no players may enter it
- Otherwise, normal football rules apply

## Progression 1
Players can cross the central zone but the ball must be played around it

## Progression 2
Players can use the central zone but are limited to two touches

## Exercise 132

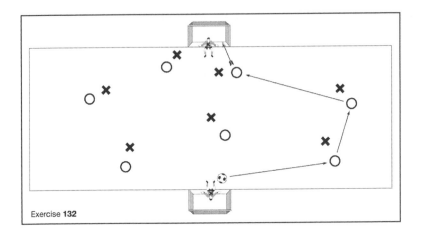

Exercise **132**

**Equipment:** 2 goals, set of bibs, balls   **No of players:** 16

**Time:** 4-8 x 8 min         **Pitch size:** 60m wide x 40m long

### The Game:
- Play 7 v 7 plus two goalkeepers
- Each team attacks and defends a goal
- If goalkeepers are not available, then the ball must hit the net off the ground for a goal to count
- The shape of the pitch should encourage wide play
- Normal goals score one point
- A header on target also counts as one point but a goal scored with the head is worth three points

## Exercise 133

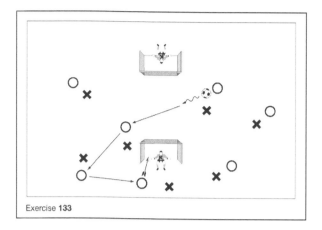

Exercise **133**

**Equipment:** 2 goals, set of bibs, balls      **No of players:** 16

**Time:** 4-8 x 8 min      **Pitch size:** 60m x 35m

**The Game:**
- Play 7 v 7 plus two goalkeepers
- The two goals, which are 30m apart, face outwards to the goal lines, as in the diagram
- Each team attacks and defends a goal
- For a goal to count, all attacking players must be in the central or attacking zone

**Progression 1**
Play offside in each attacking zone

**Progression 2**
- Both goalkeepers are neutral
- One team tries to maintain possession of the ball
- The other team tries win the ball and score in either goal
- Change roles every eight minutes

## Exercise 134

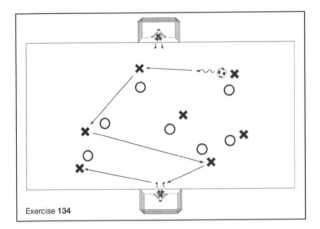

Exercise **134**

**Equipment:** 2 goals, set of bibs, balls    **No of players:** 16

**Time:** 4-8 x 8 min    **Pitch size:** 50m x 40m

**The Game:**
- Play 7 v 7 plus two neutral goalkeepers
- One team tries to maintain possession of the ball
- The other team attacks quickly and attempts to score in either goal
- After eight minutes, change roles

**Progression**
Each team attacks and defends a goal

## Exercise 135

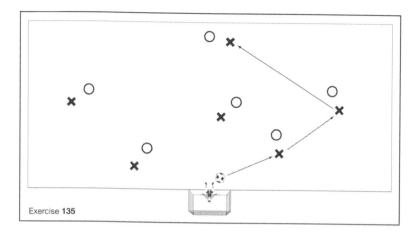

Exercise **135**

**Equipment:** 1 goal, set of bibs, balls    **No of players:** 15

**Time:** 4-8 x 8 min    **Pitch size:** 60m wide x 40m long

### The Game:
- Play 7 v 6
- The team of six attacks the normal goal and attempts to score as many goals as possible in eight minutes
- The team of seven tries to maintain possession and scores a point for ten consecutive passes
- Change roles after eight minutes

### Progression
- The team of six attacks the normal goal whilst the team of seven tries to maintain possession
- The team trying to score starts with an imaginary 3 – 0 deficit. Can they score four goals to win?

## Exercise 136

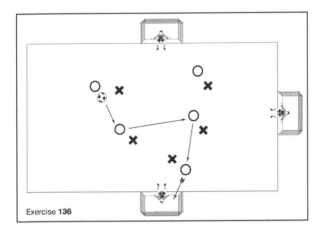

Exercise **136**

**Equipment:** 3 goals, 4 cones, set of bibs, balls  **No of players:** 13

**Time:** 4-8 x 6 min                                   **Pitch size:** 40m x 35m

**The Game:**
- Play 5 v 5 plus three goalkeepers
- One team attacks all three goals, whilst the other team tries to maintain possession
- Change roles every six minutes

**Progression**
- Each team attacks and defends the three goals
- The goalkeepers are neutral
- If the defending team wins the ball, they have to make three consecutive passes before they can shoot

# Exercise 137

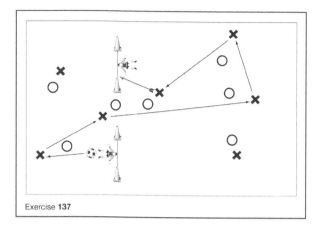

Exercise **137**

**Equipment:** 4 poles, 4 cones, set of bibs, balls     **No of players:** 16

**Time:** 4-8 x 8 min

**Pitch size:** 50m x 30m

## The Game:
- Play 7 v 7 + two goalkeepers
- Each team attacks and defends a lateral goal, as shown in the diagram
- A headed goal counts double
- Teams can score from either side of the goal

## Progression
- One team attacks both goals, whilst the other tries to maintain possession
- The attacking team starts with a 3 – 0 deficit
- Change roles after eight minutes

## Exercise 138

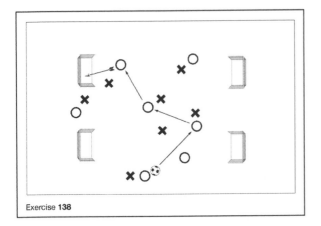

Exercise **138**

**Equipment:** 4 goals, set of bibs, balls   **No of players:** 14

**Time:** 4-8 x 8 min                        **Pitch size:** 50m x 35m

### The Game:
- Play 7 v 7
- Each team attacks and defends two lateral goals (4m)
- The finish must be one touch and the ball has to hit the net off the ground. It cannot bounce!

### Progression
Each team attacks and defends two diagonal goals

## Exercise 139

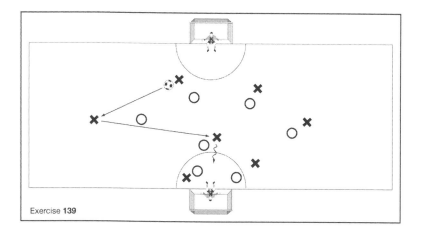

Exercise **139**

**Equipment:** 2 goals, set of bibs, balls        **No of players:** 16

**Time:** 4-8 x 8 min        **Pitch size:** 50m x 35m

### The Game:
- Play 7 v 7 + two goalkeepers
- Each team attacks and defends a goal
- In front of each goal is a shooting circle (15m radius)
- The attacking team attempts to dribble into the opponents' shooting area and then score
- Once a player has dribbled into the shooting circle, he can either shoot or pass to a team mate
- Shots from outside the area do not count
- If a player shoots from outside the circle, a free kick is given
- If the ball is passed into the circle, a free kick is given

## Exercise 140

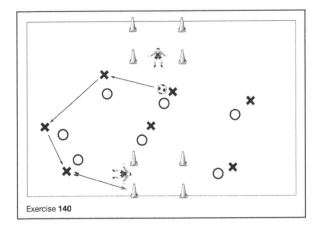

Exercise **140**

**Equipment:** 8 poles, 4 cones, set of bibs, balls   **No of players:** 16

**Time:** 4-6 x 8 min                              **Pitch size:** 50m x 30m

### The Game:
- Play 7 v 7 + two goalkeepers
- Each team attacks and defends a five-metre square, marked out with poles and defended by a goalkeeper
- The attacking team has three sides of the square to shoot at
- The finish must be one-touch

### Progression
- One team attacks both goals whilst the other tries to maintain possession
- The attacking team starts with a 3 – 0 deficit. Can they score four goals?
- Change roles after eight minutes

# Exercise 141

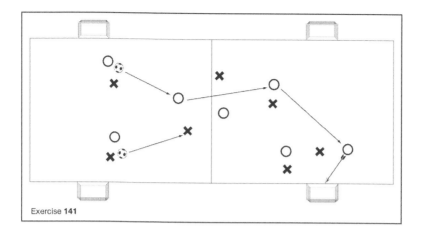

Exercise **141**

**Equipment:** 6 cones, 4 goals, set of bibs, balls   **No of players:** 14

**Time:** 4-6 x 8 min                    **Pitch size:** 50m x 40m

### The Game:
- Play 7 v 7 on four goals
- Each team attacks and defends two goals
- Players must have three touches each time they receive the ball
- Teams score with a one-touch finish

### Progression 1
To make the game more intense, use two balls

### Progression 2
- Divide the pitch into two halves
- Attackers must play the ball in both halves before they can shoot

# Exercise 142

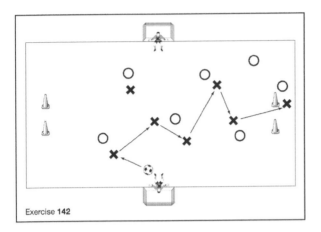

Exercise **142**

**Equipment:** 2 goals, 4 poles or cones, set of bibs, balls   **No of players:** 16

**Time:** 4-6 x 8 min                                    **Pitch size:** 50m x 35m

**The Game:**
* Play 7 v 7 + two goalkeepers
* Each team attacks and defends a normal goal and two small goals (2m) situated on the half way line, as in the diagram
* Normal scoring applies in the large goals but only a one-touch finish in the small goals

**Progression 1**
Normal scoring in the large goals, but players pass to a team mate through the small goals, to score a point

**Progression 2**
Normal scoring in the large goals, but two players perform a take over through the small goals, to score a point

## Exercise 143

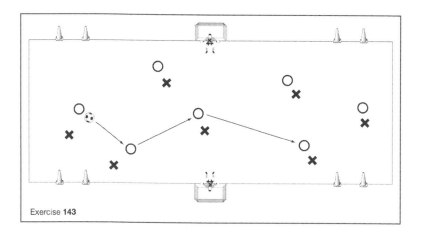

Exercise **143**

**Equipment:** 2 goals, 8 cones, set of bibs, balls   **No of players:** 16

**Time:** 4-6 x 8 min

**Pitch size:** 50m x 35m

### The Game:
- Play 7 v 7 plus two goalkeepers
- Each team attacks and defends two normal goals and two small goals (2m)
- Normal scoring applies in the large goals, but only a one-touch finish is allowed in the small goals

### Progression 1
Players dribble the ball through the small goals, with the ball under control, to score a point

### Progression 2
A headed goal counts double in the large goal

## Exercise 144

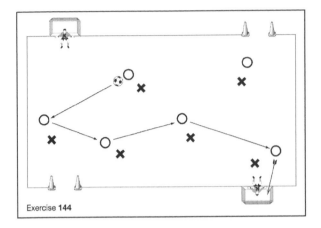

Exercise **144**

**Equipment:** 2 goals, 4 cones or poles, set of bibs, balls **No of players:** 14

**Time:** 4-6 x 8 min                                         **Pitch size:** 50m x 35m

### The Game:
- Play 7 v 7 + two goalkeepers
- Each team attacks and defends two normal goals and two small goals (2m), as shown in the diagram
- Normal scoring applies in the large goals, but only a one-touch finish is allowed in the small goals

### Progression 1
Players dribble through the small goals, with the ball under control, to score a point

### Progression 2
A headed goal counts double in the large goal

# Exercise 145

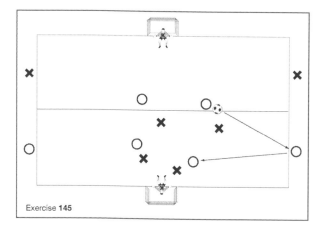

Exercise **145**

**Equipment:** 2 goals, 4 cones, set of bibs, balls   **No of players:** 14

**Time:** 6-10 x 4 min                                   **Pitch size:** 40m x 30m

## The Game:
- Play 6 v 6 + two goalkeepers
- Each team attacks and defends a normal goal
- Both teams have two resting players positioned in the attacking half of the pitch, one on each side line, as in the diagram
- The wide players have one or two touches
- If they take two touches, they must cross the ball
- Change the resting players every four minutes

## Exercise 146

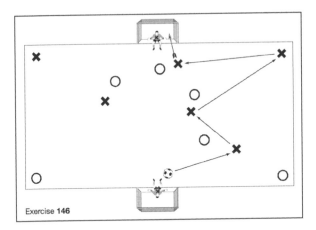

Exercise 146

**Equipment:** 2 goals, 4 cones, set of bibs, balls    **No of players:** 14

**Time:** 6-10 x 4 min                               **Pitch size:** 50m x 40m

**The Game:**
- Play 6 v 6 + two goalkeepers
- Each team attacks and defends a normal goal
- Two players from each team are placed in the corners of their attacking half of the pitch
- The team in possession tries to progress play and pass to one of their corner players
- The corner player crosses the ball for a possible shot or header at goal
- The corner player cannot be tackled
- Any goal scored from a cross counts double
- Change the corner players every four minutes

# Exercise 147

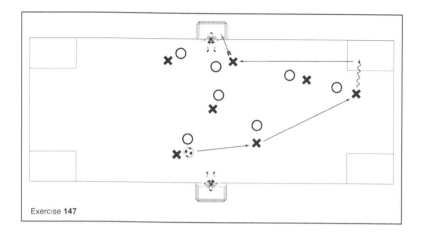

Exercise **147**

**Equipment:** 16 cones, 2 goals, set of bibs, balls    **No of players:** 16

**Time:** 4-6 x 8 min    **Pitch size:** 60m x 40m

## The Game:
- Play 7 v 7 + two goalkeepers
- Each team attacks and defends a normal goal
- Four zones (6m x 6m) are marked out in the corners of the pitch
- Defenders are not allowed in the zones
- Attackers may either pass or dribble into the zones
- Goals can only be scored after a pass from one of the marked zones
- If a strike is not made after two touches, the ball has to be crossed again from one of the zones before another shot can be taken

## Exercise 148

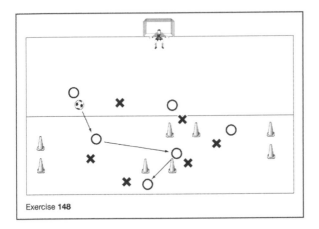

Exercise 148

**Equipment:** 8 cones, goal, set of bibs, balls     **No of players:** 13

**Time:** 4-6 x 8 min     **Pitch size:** 50m x 35m

### The Game:
- Play 6 v 6 + one goalkeeper
- One team (O) defends a normal goal whilst the other team (X) defends four small goals (2m) randomly placed on the other half of the pitch
- Team O has to maintain possession of the ball and advance quickly into the opponents' half
- Here they attempt to pass the ball to a team mate through one of the small goals
- Team X tries to win the ball and progress quickly into the opponents' half
- Here they attempt to score in the normal goal
- After eight minutes the teams change roles

### Progression 1
The team attacking the four small goals scores a point each time a player dribbles through a goal and successfully passes to a team mate

### Progression 2
The team attacking the four small goals scores a point every time two players perform a take over in any of the goals

## Exercise 149

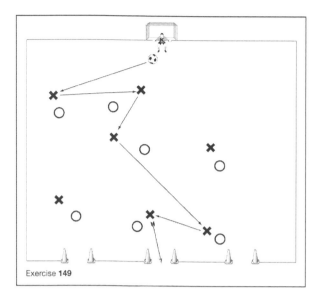

Exercise **149**

**Equipment:** 6 cones or poles, goal, set of bibs, balls  **No of players:** 15

**Time:** 4-6 x 8 min                                      **Pitch size:** Half a pitch

**The Game:**
- Play 7 v 7 + a goalkeeper
- One team attacks three small goals (3m) placed on the half-way line, whilst the other team attacks the normal goal
- After eight minutes, the teams reverse roles

**Progression** 1
Only goals scored in the normal goal count towards the final score
When a team scores in one of the small goals, it can then attack the normal goal

**Progression** 2
- Divide the pitch into two
- The team attacking the large goal only wins a point if they score and all their players are in the opponents' half of the field
- The team attacking the three small goals only wins a point if they score and all their players are in the opponents' half of the field

## Exercise 150

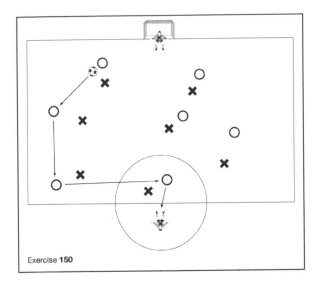

Exercise **150**

**Equipment:** 1 goal, set of bibs, balls    **No of players:** 16

**Time:** 4-6 x 8 min    **Pitch size:** Half a pitch

### The Game:
- Play 7 v 7 plus two goalkeepers
- One goalkeeper defends the normal goal, whilst the other stands inside the centre circle, behind the half-way line
- One team attacks the goal, whilst the other tries to cross the ball for a header to the goalkeeper in the centre circle
- Teams change roles after eight minutes

### Progression
The team defending the normal goal scores a point if, after making five consecutive passes, they play the ball to the goalkeeper standing in the centre circle

# Exercise 151

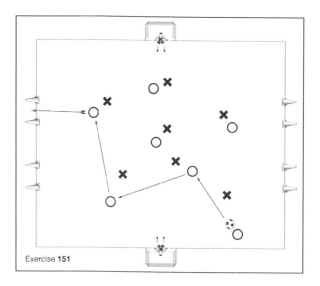

Exercise **151**

**Equipment:** 8 cones or poles, 2 goals, set of bibs, balls  **No of players:** 16

**Time:** 4 x 10 min                                                    **Pitch size:** 60m x 40m

## The Game:
- Play 9 v 7
- One team attacks the normal goals, with goalkeepers, and defends the four small goals (2m) situated on the sides of the pitch.
- The other team attacks the four small goals and defends the two normal goals
- It must be a one-touch finish in the small goals
- When in possession, both teams attempt to attack the opponents' goals as quickly as possible
- Teams change roles after 10 minutes

# Exercise 152

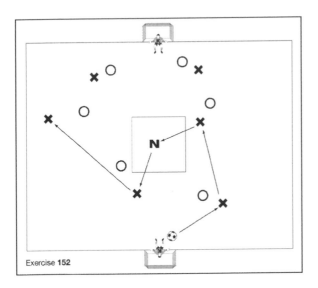

Exercise 152

**Equipment:** 8 cones, set of bibs, two goals, balls    **No of players:** 15

**Time:** 4-6 x 8 min                                          **Pitch size:** 50m x 40m

## The Game:
- Play 7 v 7 + one neutral player
- Each team attacks and defends a goal
- Mark out a 7m square in the middle of the pitch
- The neutral player is placed in the square and can help whichever team has the ball
- Teams should look for wall passes with the neutral player
- No other player can enter the central square

## Progression
- The neutral player moves around the pitch and plays for the team in possession
- However, he is the only player that can enter the central square, but is limited to two touches

# Exercise 153

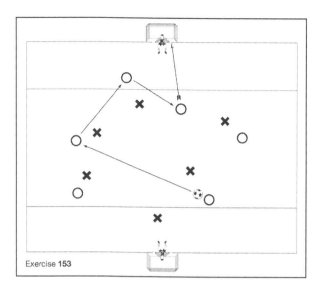

Exercise 153

**Equipment:** 8 cones, 2 goals, set of bibs, balls     **No of players:** 14

**Time:**  4-6 x 6 min

**Pitch size:** 60m x 35m

## The Game:
- Play 6 v 6 + two goalkeepers
- A zone (10m by 35m) is marked out in front of both goals
- Each team puts one player in their attacking zone, as in the diagram
- No other player is allowed in the zone
- Each team attacks and defends one goal
- To score, the attacking team has to pass to their player in the zone
- This player has two touches to set the ball up for a team mate to shoot from outside the zone

## Exercise 154

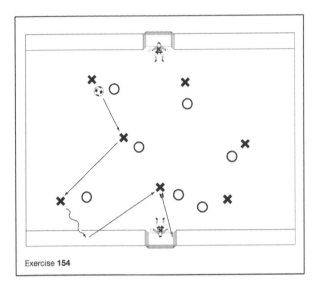

Exercise **154**

**Equipment:** 2 goals, set of bibs, balls    **No of players:** 16

**Time:** 4-6 x 8 min                 **Pitch size:** 50m x 35m

**The Game:**
- Play 7 v 7 + two goalkeepers
- Each team attacks and defends a normal goal
- The attacking team can only score from a cut back, as in the diagram
- Players who take shots which are not from cut backs are penalised by a free kick

**Progression**
- Two zones, 5m x 35m, are created behind the goals
- The ball has to be passed from this zone, behind the goal, before an attacker can shoot

# Exercise 155

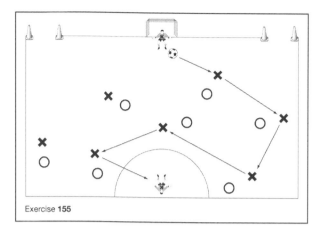

Exercise **155**

**Equipment:** 4 cones or poles, goal, set of bibs, balls  **No of players:** 16

**Time:** 4-6 x 10 min                              **Pitch size:** Half a pitch

**The Game:**
- Play 7 v 7 + two goalkeepers
- One team attacks a normal goal, with a goalkeeper, and two small goals (2m) placed on the corners of the goal line
- The finish must be one-touch in the small goals
- The team defending the normal goal and small goals must make five consecutive passes and then play to the goalkeeper standing in the centre circle, to score a point.
- The teams change roles every 10 minutes

**Progression**
When the team successfully passes to the goalkeeper in the centre circle, they immediately attack in the opposite direction

## Exercise 156

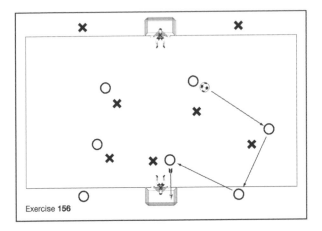

Exercise **156**

**Equipment:** 2 goals, 4 cones, set of bibs, balls   **No of players:** 16

**Time:** 4-8 x 5 min                                    **Pitch size:** 50m x 30m

### The Game:
- Play 7 v 7 + two goalkeepers
- Each team attacks and defends a normal goal
- Both teams have two lay-off players positioned behind the goal line, in the attacking half of the field
- These players can move up and down the goal line, but cannot move on to the field
- Each team scores a point for a normal goal but two points if the ball is played to a lay-off player and then passed back for a team mate to score
- Change the lay-off players every five minutes

### Progression 1
Restrict the lay-off players to one touch

### Progression 2
A headed goal from a pass by a lay-off player scores three points

## Exercise 157

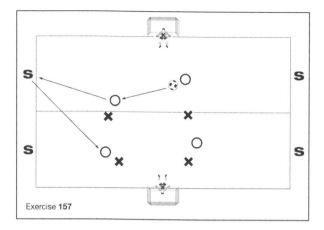

Exercise 157

**Equipment:** 2 goals, set of bibs, balls

**No of players:** 14

**Time:** 6 x 4 min

**Pitch size:** 40m x 30m

**The Game:**
- Play 4 v 4 + 4 and two goalkeepers
- Each team attacks and defends a normal goal
- Four lay-off players are situated on the touch lines (as in the diagram) and play with the team in possession
- The lay-off players cannot be tackled but are restricted to one or two touches
- Rotate the players every four minutes

**Progression**
- The team that scores stays on the pitch but has to sprint to the goal they are defending before rejoining the game
- The team that conceded the goal sprints to the side and become lay-off players
- The lay-off players sprint on to the pitch and become attackers

## Exercise 158

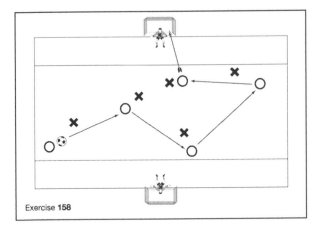

Exercise **158**

**Equipment:** 8 cones, 2 goals, set of bibs, balls    **No of players:** 12

**Time:** 6-8 x 4 min                                **Pitch size:** 50m x 30m

**The Game:**
- Play 5 v 5 plus two goalkeepers
- Each team attacks and defends a normal goal
- A zone (10m x 30m) is marked out in front of each goal
- The players are restricted to the central zone (30m by 30m)
- The attacking team tries to move the ball quickly and shoot at the opponents' goal
- Play is limited to two touches and all shots must be taken from the central zone

## Exercise 159

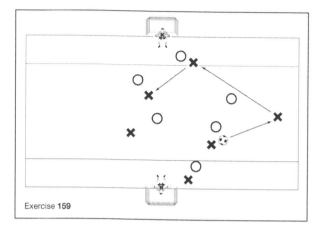

Exercise **159**

**Equipment:** 8 cones, 2 goals, set of bibs, balls    **No of players:** 14

**Time:** 4-6 x 8 min    **Pitch size:** 50m x 30m

**The Game:**
- Play 6 v 6 + two goalkeepers
- Each team attacks ands defends a normal goal
- The field is divided into three: a central zone (30m by 30m) and two outer zones (10m by 30m)
- Each team places one player in their defensive zone, four in the central zone and one in the attacking zone
- The team in possession tries to progress play quickly and shoot at the opponents' goal from the central zone
- However, goals can only be scored by a set up ball from the player in the attacking zone
- The attacking player can follow up any shot from the central zone and shoot, if the goalkeeper drops the ball
- If the defender wins the ball, he immediately passes to his team in the central zone
- Change the players in the attacking and defending zones every eight minutes

## Exercise 160

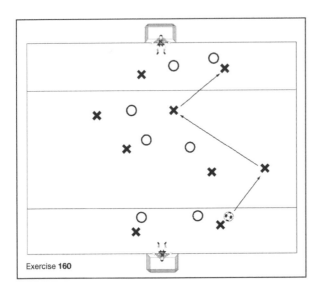

Exercise **160**

**Equipment:** 8 cones, 2 goals, set of bibs, balls    **No of players:** 18

**Time:** 4-6 x 8 min    **Pitch size:** 60m x 35m

**The Game:**
- Play 8 v 8 + two goalkeepers
- Both teams attack and defend a normal goal
- There are two outside zones (15m by 35m) and a central zone (30m by 35m)
- Each team has two players in the defensive zone, four in the central zone, and two in the attacking zone
- The team in possession tries to pass to one of their players in the attacking zone
- This player can shoot or pass to his team mate if he is in a better position
- Players have to remain in their own zones
- After eight minutes, the players change zones

# Exercise 161

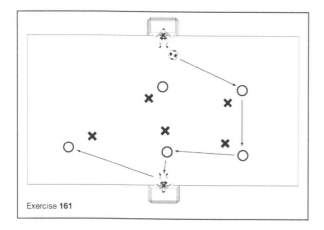

Exercise **161**

**Equipment:** 2 goals, set of bibs, balls   **No of players:** 12

**Time:** 4-6 x 5 min

**Pitch size:** 40 x 35m

### The Game:
- Play 5 v 5 + two neutral goalkeepers
- One team tries to maintain possession of the ball, with the help of the two goalkeepers.
- The other team tries to move the ball quickly and score as many times as possible in either of the goals
- Every six minutes change the roles of the teams

## Exercise 162

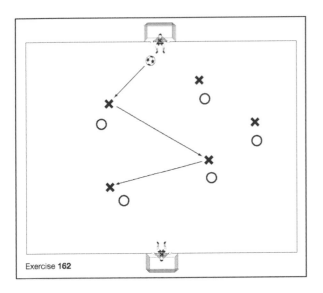

Exercise 162

**Equipment:** 2 goals, set of bibs, balls     **No of players:** 12

**Time:** 4-6 x 5 min                          **Pitch size:** 40m x 30m

### The Game:
- Play 5 v 5 + two goalkeepers
- Each team attacks and defends a normal goal
- One team (X) is told that it is leading 1-0 with five minutes of the match remaining
- Both teams, therefore, have to work out their tactics for the match situation
- Team X has to maintain possession of the ball, whilst team O has to press for an equaliser
- The teams change roles every five minutes

# Exercise 163

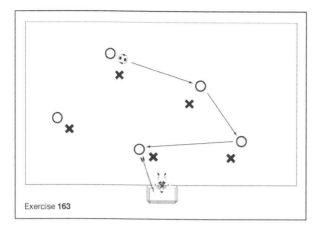

Exercise **163**

**Equipment:** 1 goal, set of bibs, balls

**No of players:** 11

**Time:** 4 x 6 min

**Pitch size:** 40m x 30m

## The Game:

- Play 5 v 5 + one goalkeeper
- Team O attacks a normal goal and is told that they are 2-0 down with six minutes left
- The other team (X) defending the goal is told that they are leading 2- 0
- Both teams have to work out their tactics for the final six minutes
- Team X attempts to keep possession and slow the game down
- Team O tries to recover the two-goal deficit

## Exercise 164

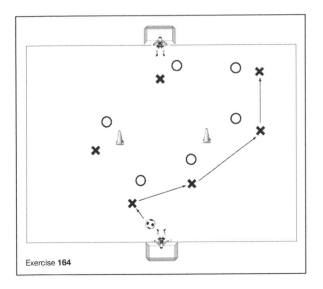

Exercise 164

**Equipment:** 2 goals, 2 cones, set of bibs, balls  **No of players:** 14

**Time:** 4-6 x 8 min  **Pitch size:** 50m x 35m

**The Game:**
- Play 6 v 6 + two goalkeepers
- Each team attacks and defends a goal
- A 15-metre space is marked out in the middle of the field, as in the diagram
- The ball must not be played through this space, although players can run through it
- Any infringement results in a free kick for the opposition
- The aim is to encourage wide play by the team in possession

# Exercise 165

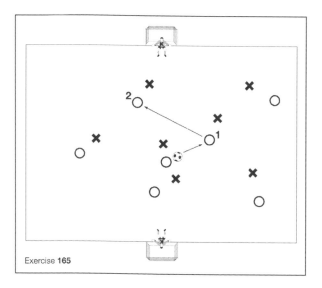

Exercise 165

**Equipment:** 2 goals, 4 cones, set of bibs, balls    **No of players:** 16

**Time:** 4-6 x 8 min    **Pitch size:** 50m x 40m

## The Game:
- Play 7 v 7 + two goalkeepers
- Each team attacks and defends a goal
- If the defenders win the ball, the NEXT two players are each limited to two touches
- Keeping the ball is now a priority
- Players should spread out and show for the ball

## Exercise 166

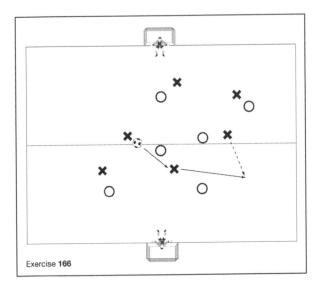

Exercise **166**

**Equipment:** 2 goals, 2 cones, set of bibs, balls    **No of players:** 14

**Time:** 4-6 x 8 min                                    **Pitch size:** 50m x 30m

- **The Game**
- Play 6 v 6 + two goalkeepers
- The field is divided into two halves
- Each team attacks and defends a goal, and places two players in their defensive zone and two in their attacking zone
- In addition, there are two midfield players who can play in either zone
- The midfield players act as the link between the two fields of play
- After eight minutes, everybody changes roles

## Exercise 167

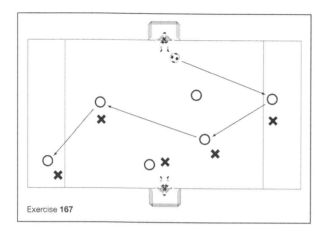

Exercise 167

**Equipment:** 2 goals, 8 cones, set of bibs, balls    **No of players:** 14

**Time:** 4-6 x 6 min                                  **Pitch size:** 50m x 40m

**The Game:**
Play 6 v 6 + two goalkeepers
- The field is divided into three zones: two narrow lateral zones (5m by 50m) and a central zone (30m by 50m)
- Each team attacks and defends a normal goal
- Only one player from each team can enter a lateral zone at any one time
- He should then dribble the ball at pace in order to create a fast finish
- Shots can only be taken after a cross from a lateral zone

## Exercise 168

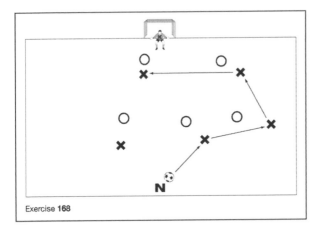

Exercise 168

**Equipment:** 1 goal, 4 cones, set of bibs, balls    **No of players:** 12

**Time:** 4-6 x 5 min                                    **Pitch size:** Half a pitch

**The Game:**
- Play 5 v 5 + one neutral player + one goalkeeper
- Play the width of the penalty area
- One team attacks a normal goal with a goalkeeper
- The defending team tries to win the ball and then passes to the neutral player, who is standing on the half-way line
- The offensive players still attempt to regain possession before the ball reaches the neutral player
- If the defending team manages to get the ball to the neutral player, he passes back to the defenders and they become the attackers
- Change the neutral player every five minutes

# Exercise 169

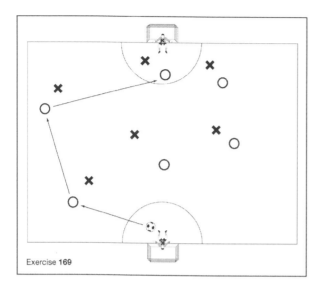

Exercise **169**

**Equipment:** 2 goals, 8 cones, set of bibs, balls    **No of players:** 12

**Time:** 4-6 x 6 min    **Pitch size:** 50m x 35m

## The Game:
- Play 6 v 6 plus two goalkeepers
- Each team attacks and defends a goal
- In front of each goal is a heading circle, with a 10-metre radius
- Goals inside the circle must be scored with the head
- Outside the circle, goals can be scored in any way

## Progression
Goals can only be scored with a header or volley, inside the circle

## Exercise 170

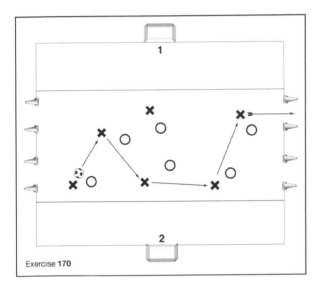

Exercise 170

**Equipment:** 2 goals, 16 cones, set of bibs, balls   **No of players:** 14

**Time:** 4 x 8 min                              **Pitch size:** 50m x 40m

**The Game:**
- Play 7 v 7
- A playing area 50m x 40m is divided into three zones
- In the central zone (30m x 40m) each team attacks and defends two small goals, as in the diagram
- All players must stay in the central zone
- On a signal from the coach, the teams switch to using the three zones and attack and defend the large goals
- Teams score with a one-touch finish
- Neither team knows which goal they will be attacking or defending until the coach calls out a direction
- After a few min the teams revert back to working in the central zone and attacking and defending the small goals

**Progression**
- Both teams play 'keep ball' in the central zone
- On a signal from the coach, the team in possession switches to attacking goal 1
- After four minutes, teams revert back to 'keep ball' in the central zone

# Exercise 171

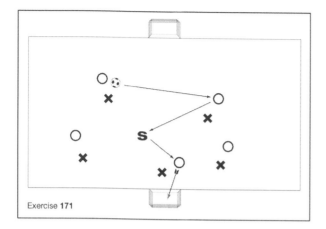

Exercise 171

**Equipment:** 2 goals, 4 cones, set of bibs     **No of players:** 11

**Time:** 5 x 5 min

**Pitch size:** 50m x 30m

## The Game:
- Play 5 v 5 plus one support player, who wears a different coloured bib
- The support player always plays for the team in possession
- However, the only player who can score is the support player or a player to whom the support player has passed
- Change the support player every five minutes with a member of the winning team

## Progression
- Play 5 v 5 with one player from each team chosen as a target man
- Both target men wear different coloured bibs
- The only player who can score is the target player or a player to whom the target player has passed
- Allow both teams time to work out their tactics

Chapter 13

# Defending from the Front

### Exercise 172

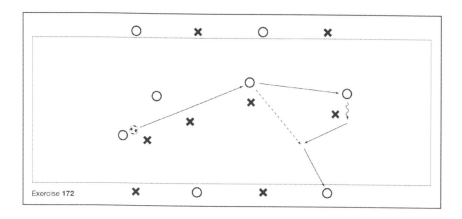

Exercise 172

**Equipment:** 4 cones, 2 sets of bibs, balls    **No of players:** 16

**Time:** 6 x 5 min                              **Pitch size:** 40m x 30m

**The Game:**
* Divide players into two teams of eight
* Four players from each team are positioned on the field and two on each side line
* Attackers try to keep possession and pass to a team mate on the side line
* If successful, they start a new attack in the opposite direction
* Outside players are limited to one touch
* The defending team attempts to stop forward passes and pressure the ball whenever possible
* Change the side players every five minutes

**Progression**
* Whoever passes to the side player takes his place
* However, the attackers have to make a minimum of three passes before they can pass to an opposite side player

## Exercise 173

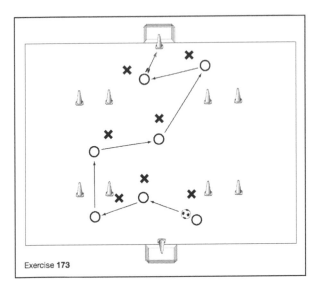

Exercise 173

**Equipment:** 12 cones, 2 sets of bibs, 2 goals, balls  **No of players:** 14

**Time:** 4 x 8 min                                    **Pitch size:** 60m x 40m

### The Game:

- Play 7 v 7 with a goal at each end
- Using cones, set up four two-metre goals, as in the diagram
- Teams score two points by striking a cone placed in the middle of the end goal that they are attacking
- They also score one point if they can pass the ball through either of the two-metre goals closest to the goal they are defending
- This forces the defending team to apply pressure high up the field

### Progression

- The team in possession may score through any of the four goals to win a point
- This will force the defending team to apply pressure all over the field, in order to keep the attackers from scoring

# Exercise 174

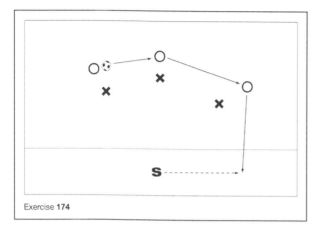

Exercise **174**

**Equipment:** 6 cones, set of bibs, balls   **No of players:** 7

**Time:** 8 x 4 min                          **Pitch size:** 20m square

## The Game:

- Play 3 v 3 plus one support player
- The support player is placed in a five-metre zone, as in the diagram
- He is free to move anywhere in the zone, where he cannot be tackled
- The aim is for the attacking team to make a minimum of three passes before attempting to pass to the support player
- If successful, the attacking team scores one point
- The ball is then returned to the attacking team by the support player and the process starts again
- The defending team tries to apply pressure all over the field, in order to prevent the attackers from scoring
- If the defenders win the ball, roles change and they become the attackers
- They now have to make a minimum of three passes before they can pass to the support player
- After four minutes, a player from the losing team changes place with the support player

## Exercise 175

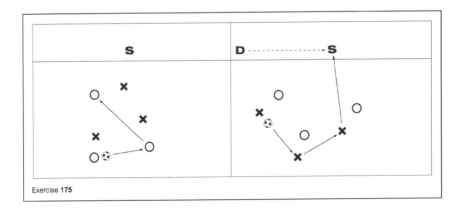

Exercise 175

**Equipment:** 8 cones, balls, 2 sets of bibs  **No of players:** 15

**Time:** 8 x 4 min  **Pitch size:** 2 x 20m squares

### The Game:
- Play 2 x 3 v 3 in two marked fields, as in the diagram
- Adjoining both fields is a five-metre support zone
- Place one support player at each end of the five-metre zone. There is also one defender – who can work anywhere in this zone
- The aim is for the attacking team on both fields to make a minimum of three passes before passing to their support player in the five-metre zone
- They score one point if they pass to the support player and he returns the ball to them
- If the defender intercepts or successfully tackles the support player, then a point is not awarded
- The defending team should apply pressure all over the field in order to prevent the attackers from scoring
- If the defenders win the ball, roles change and they become the at-tackers
- They now have to make a minimum of three passes before they can pass to the support player
- After four minutes, change the defender and support players

## Exercise 176

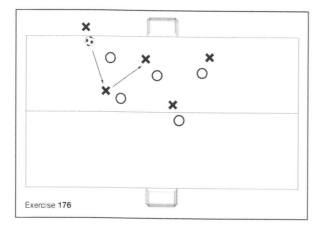

Exercise **176**

**Equipment:** 4 cones, 2 goals, set of bibs, balls   **No of players:** 10

**Time:** 6 x 5 min                              **Pitch size:** 50m x 40m

**The Game:**
- Play 5 v 5
- Each team attacks and defends a goal
- Teams score by hitting the net off the ground
- If a team scores, their opponents restart the game from their own goal line
- If the scoring team doesn't get the ball back within five passes, then the goal does NOT count
- The scoring team needs to apply pressure all over the field, in order to prevent the attackers from making five passes

## Exercise 177

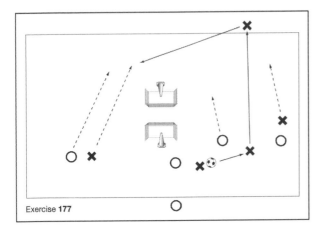

Exercise **177**

**Equipment:** 6 cones, 2 small goals, set of bibs, balls **No of players:** 10

**Time:** 6 x 5 min                                        **Pitch size:** 40m x 30m

**The Game:**
- Play 5 v 5
- A support player from each team stands on the opposition's goal line
- When the ball is won in the defending half of the field, the ball must be passed as quickly as possible to the support player standing on the opposition's goal line
- Whoever passes to the support player takes his place
- The attackers now try to maintain possession and strike a cone placed in the middle of the goal they are attacking
- They can use their support player in order to keep possession
- The support player cannot be tackled. Whoever passes to the support player takes his place
- The defending team must apply pressure in the defensive half of the field in order to win the ball and pass to their support player in the opposite half
- When possession changes, the teams must respond immediately

# Exercise 178

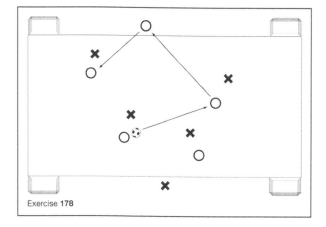

Exercise **178**

**Equipment:** 10 cones, set of bibs, balls      **No of players:** 10

**Time:** 6 x 5 min      **Pitch size:** 40m x 20m

**The Game:**
- Play 5 v 5
- Two small goals are placed on each goal line, as in the diagram
- A support player from each team stands on the opposition's goal line
- When the ball is won in the defending half of the field, the ball must be passed as quickly as possible to the support player standing on the opposition's goal line
- Whoever passes to the support player, takes his place. The support player cannot be tackled
- The attackers score by dribbling through either of their opponents' goals, once they have received a pass from the support player
- They can use their support player in order to keep possession
- The defending team must apply pressure in their defensive half of the field, in order to win the ball and pass to their support player in the opposite half
- When possession changes, both teams must respond immediately

## Exercise 179

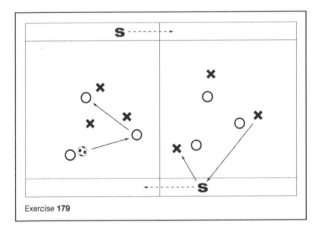

Exercise 179

**Equipment:** 10 cones, balls, 2 sets of bibs   **No of players:** 14

**Time:** 8 x 4 min                              **Pitch size:** 2 x 20m squares

**The Game:**
- Play 2 x 3 v 3 in two marked areas, as in the diagram
- A five-metre free zone is marked out at either end of the pitch
- A support player is placed in each free zone but has to assist in BOTH games
- The attacking team scores a point if they pass to a support player and then work the ball to the other support player
- As the support players are working in both games, the attacking team might have to be patient, until a support player becomes available
- The defending teams should apply pressure all over the field, in order to prevent their opponents from scoring
- If the defenders win the ball, roles change and they become the attackers
- After four minutes, change the support players

# Exercise 180

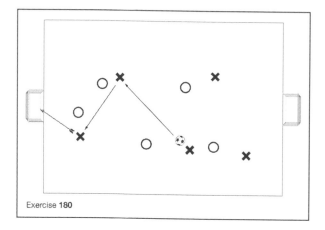

Exercise **180**

**Equipment:** 4 cones, 2 goals, set of bibs, balls   **No of players:** 10

**Time:** 6 x 5 min                                                            **Pitch size:** 50m x 40m

## The Game:
- Play 5 v 5
- Each team attacks and defends a goal
- Teams score by hitting the net off the ground
- After a team scores, the NEXT team to score gets the point
- Once a goal is scored, both teams have to apply pressure all over the pitch in order to prevent the opposition scoring the second goal
- Once the second goal has been scored, both teams start again at 0-0

## Exercise 181

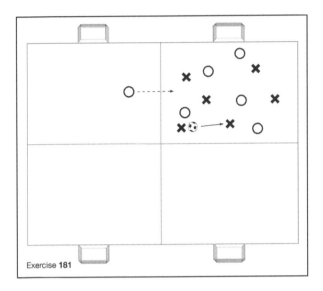

Exercise **181**

**Equipment:** 4 goals, 9 cones, set of bibs, balls  **No of players:** 12

**Time:** 6 x 5 min                                    **Pitch size:** 60m x 50m

### The Game:
- Play 6 v 6
- Divide the field into four equal quarters of 30m x 25m, with two goals on each side
- Each team attacks and defends two goals
- ALL attackers have to be in the quarter of the field in which the goal is scored
- If an attacker is not in that quarter of the field, then the goal does not count
- If one of the defenders is not in that quarter of the field, then the goal counts double
- If the attackers lose possession in their attacking half of the field, then they must apply immediate pressure to win the ball back
- This is a physically demanding game, so allow several minutes rest between games

# Exercise 182

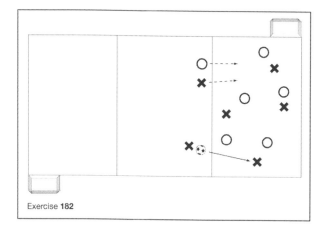

Exercise **182**

**Equipment:** 2 goals, 8 cones, set of bibs, balls   **No of players:** 12

**Time:** 6 x 5 min                                    **Pitch size:** 60m x 30m

**The Game:**
- Play 6 v 6
- Divide the field into three equal zones (30m x 20m), with a goal in each outside zone, as shown in the diagram
- Each team attacks and defends one goal
- If a team scores, the goal only counts if ALL the attackers are in their attacking zone
- If one of the defenders is not in their defensive zone when a goal is scored, then the goal counts double
- If the attackers lose possession in their attacking third, then they must apply immediate pressure to try to win the ball back
- This is a physically demanding game, so allow several minutes rest between games

## Exercise 183

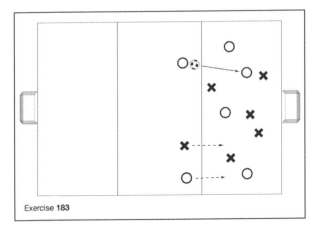

Exercise **183**

**Equipment:** 2 goals, 8 cones, set of bibs, balls   **No of players:** 12

**Time:** 6 x 5 min                              **Pitch size:** 60m x 30m

### The Game:
- Play 6 v 6
- Divide the field into three equal zones (30m x 20m), with a goal on each end line, as in the diagram
- Each team attacks and defends one goal
- If a team scores, the goal only counts if ALL the attackers are in their attacking zone
- If one of the defenders is not in their defensive zone when a goal is scored, then the goal counts double
- If the attackers lose possession in their attacking third, then they must apply immediate pressure to try to win the ball back
- This is a physically demanding game, so allow several minutes rest between games

# Exercise 184

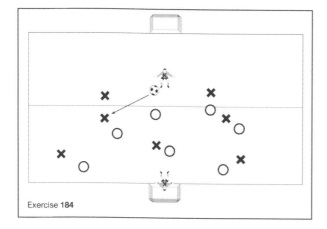

Exercise 184

**Equipment:** 2 goals, 4 cones, set of bibs, balls  **No of players:** 16

**Time:** 4 x 8 min        **Pitch size:** 60m x 40m

**The Game:**
- Play 7 v 7 plus two goalkeepers
- The goalkeeper of one team acts as a sweeper and may not use his hands
- The opposing team can score by shooting from long distance into an empty net
- The team with the sweeper must try to exert pressure from the front, in order to prevent the opposition shooting from distance
- In order to be successful, both teams will need to make a fast transition from defence to attack after winning possession
- After eight minutes teams change roles

## Exercise 185

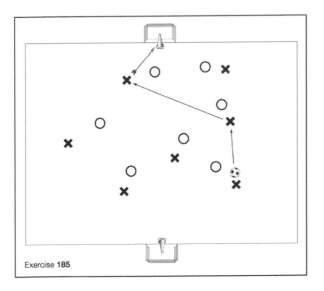

Exercise 185

**Equipment:** 2 goals, set of bibs, 6 cones, balls   **No of players:** 14

**Time:** 4 x 8 min                                          **Pitch size:** 60m x 40m

### The Game:
*   Play 7 v 7
*   Teams score by striking a large cone placed in the middle of each goal
*   When a team scores, they must score again, before the opposition, for the goal to count
*   If the opposition scores the next goal, then the game goes back to 0-0 and the process starts again
*   Pressure has to be applied all over the field by both teams, once a goal has been scored, in order to win the ball and score the crucial second goal

## Chapter 14

# Switching Games

## Exercise 186

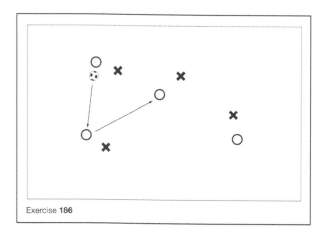

Exercise 186

**Equipment:** 4 cones, set of bibs, balls

**No of players:** 8

**Time:** 20 min

**Pitch size:** 25m x 20m

### Game One
- Play 4 v 4 keep ball
- Each team attempts to keep the ball when in possession
- There are no restrictions

### Game Two
- Play 4 v 4 keep ball
- Players are limited to three touches
- A free kick is awarded if a player has more than three touches

### Game Three
- Play 4 v 4 keep ball
- Players mark man to man
- Each pair can only defend against each other

### Switching Games
- Once players have experienced the three games, the coach randomly calls out a number and the players quickly switch to that game i.e. if

265

the coach calls out '1', the teams play 4 v 4 with no restrictions; if the coach calls out '2', players are limited to three touches and if the coach calls out '3', players mark man to man

- The coach should change games quickly in order to make players think

## Exercise 187

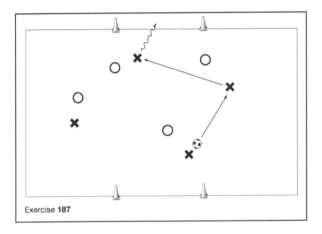

Exercise **187**

**Equipment:** 8 cones, set of bibs, balls       **No of players:** 8

**Time:** 20 min                                 **Pitch size:** 25m x 20m

### Game One
- Play 4 v 4
- Each team attacks and defends a 10-metre goal
- Teams score by stopping the ball on the goal line, with the ball under control
- There are no restrictions

### Game Two
- Play 4 v 4
- Each team attacks and defends a 10-metre goal
- Teams score by stopping the ball on the goal line, with the ball under control
- Players are restricted to three touches
- A free kick is awarded if a player has more than three touches

### Game Three
- Play 4 v 4

266

- Each team attacks and defends a 10-metre goal
- Teams score by stopping the ball on the goal line, with the ball under control
- Players mark man to man
- Each pair can only defend against each other

## Switching Games

- Once players have experienced the three games, the coach randomly calls out a number, as in exercise 186, and the players quickly switch to that game
- The coach should change games quickly in order to make players think

## Exercise 188

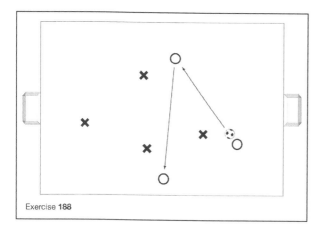

Exercise **188**

**Equipment:** 4 cones, 2 goals, set of bibs, balls    **No of players:** 8

**Time:** 20 min                                        **Pitch size:** 25m x 20m

## Game One

- Play 4 v 4
- Each team attacks and defends a goal
- Teams score by hitting the net off the ground
- There are no restrictions

## Game Two

- Play 4 v 4
- Each team attacks and defends a goal
- Teams score by hitting the net off the ground
- Players are restricted to three touches

- A free kick is awarded if a player has more than three touches

## Game Three
- Play 4 v 4
- Each team attacks and defends a goal
- Teams score by hitting the net off the ground
- Players mark man to man
- Each pair can only defend against each other

## Switching Games
- Once players have experienced the three games, the coach randomly calls out a number and the players quickly switch to that game, as in exercises 186 and 187
- The coach should change games quickly in order to make players think

## Exercise 189

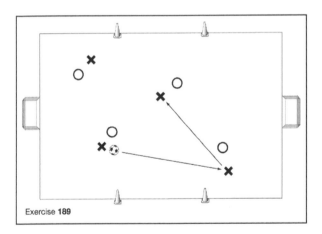

Exercise 189

**Equipment:** 8 cones, 2 goals, set of bibs, balls   **No of players:** 8

**Time:** 20 min                          **Pitch size:** 20m x 20m

## Game One
- Play 4 v 4 keep ball
- Each team attempts to keep the ball when in possession
- There are no touch restrictions

## Game Two
- Play 4 v 4
- Each team attacks and defends a 10-metre goal

- Teams score by stopping the ball on the goal line, with the ball under control
- There are no touch restrictions

## Game Three
- Play 4 v 4
- Each team attacks and defends a goal
- Teams score by hitting the net off the ground
- There are no touch restrictions

## Switching Games
- Once players have experienced the three games, the coach randomly calls out a number and the players quickly switch to that game, as in exercises 186, 187 and 188
- The coach should change games quickly in order to make players think

## Exercise 190

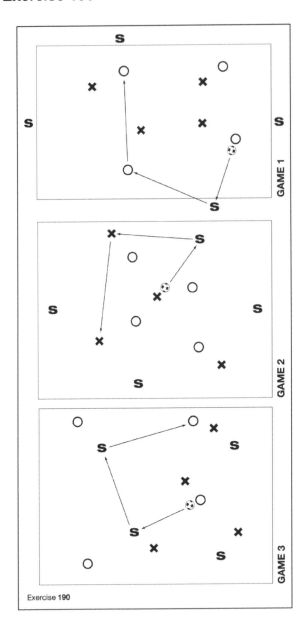

Exercise 190

**Equipment:** 4 cones, three sets of bibs, balls    **No of players:** 12

**Time:** 24 min    **Pitch size:** 20m square

## Game One
- Play 4 v 4 + 4
- X's v O's with S's acting as support on the OUTSIDE of the square, as in diagram 1
- S's can move up and down their side of the square
- The outside players cannot be tackled and support the team in possession
- The support players are limited to two touches
- Change the support players every three min

## Game Two
- Play 4 v 4 + 4
- X's v O's with S's acting as support on the INSIDE of the square, as in diagram 1
- S's can move up and down their side of the square
- The support players cannot be tackled and play for the team in possession
- The support players are limited to two touches
- Change the support players every three min

## Game Three
- Play 4 v 4 + 4
- X's v O's with S's supporting the team in possession
- S's can move ANYWHERE inside the square, creating an 8 v 4 situation, as in diagram 3
- The support players are limited to two touches
- Change the support players every three min

## Switching Games
- Once players have experienced the three different games, the coach randomly calls out a number and the players quickly switch to that game, as in exercises 186 to 189
- The coach should change games quickly in order to make players think

## Exercise 191

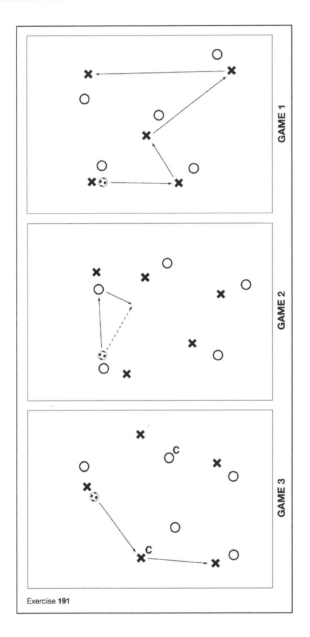

Exercise 191

**Equipment:** 4 cones, set of bibs, balls     **No of players:** 10

**Time:** 24 min     **Pitch size:** 30m square

**Game One**
- Play 5 v 5
- The attacking team tries to maintain possession of the ball
- They score a point if the ball is passed to every member of the team without the opposition intercepting it

**Game Two**
- Play 5 v 5
- The attacking team tries to maintain possession of the ball
- They score a point for every successful wall pass that is made with a team mate

**Game Three**
- Play 5 v 5
- Each team names a captain
- The attacking team tries to maintain possession of the ball
- They score a point every time the captain receives the ball and success-fully passes to a teammate

**Switching Games**
- Once players have experienced the three different games, the coach randomly calls out a number and the players quickly switch to that game, as in exercises 186 to 190
- The coach should change games quickly in order to make players think

# Exercise 192

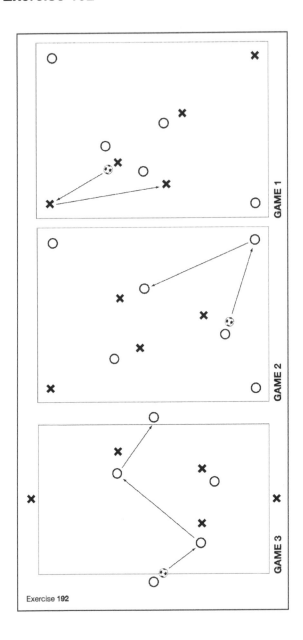

Exercise 192

**Equipment:** 4 cones, set of bibs, balls        **No of players:** 10

**Time:** 24 min        **Pitch size:** 20m square

**Game One**
- Play 5 v 5
- Each team has two support players situated in the corners of the square and three players on the field. See diagram 1
- Each team attacks and tries to maintain possession of the ball, with the help of their support players
- A team scores a point for six consecutive passes
- Change the support players every three min

**Game Two**
- Play 5 v 5
- Each team has two support players situated in the corners of the square and three players on the field. See diagram 2
- Each team attacks and tries to maintain possession of the ball with the help of all the support players
- If the ball is passed to an opposition support player, that player must return the ball to the team that passed to him
- If an outfield player passes to his own support player, the two change places
- A team scores a point for six consecutive passes

**Game Three**
- Play 5 v 5
- Each team has two support players on opposite sides of the square and three players on the field. See diagram 3
- The support players can move up and down their side
- Each team attacks and tries to maintain possession of the ball, with the help of their support players
- A team scores a point for six consecutive passes
- Change the support players every three min

**Switching Games**
- Once players have experienced the three different games, the coach randomly calls out a number and the players quickly switch to that game, as in exercises 186 to 191
- The coach should change the games quickly in order to make players think

## Exercise 193

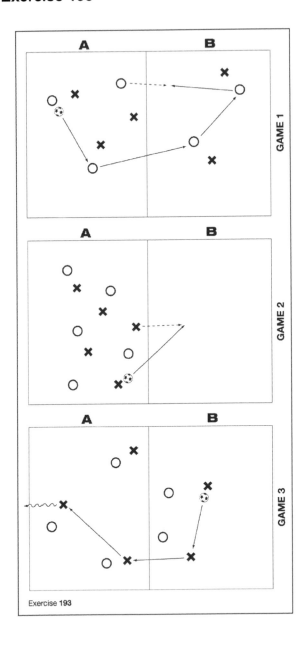

Exercise 193

**Equipment:** 6 cones, balls and set of bibs     **No of players:** 10

**Time:** 24 min     **Pitch size:** 40m x 35m

## Game One
- Play 5 v 5
- Both teams are allowed  three touches in zone A and unlimited touches in zone B
- Teams score one point for six consecutive passes
- However, all the passes cannot be in one zone

## Game Two
- O's attempt to keep the ball in zone A and score a point for six consecutive passes
- X's attempt to win the ball in zone A and take it back to zone B
- Here they score a point for six consecutive passes

## Game Three
- X's attack the end line in zone A
- They score a point by stopping the ball on the end line, under control
- O's attack the end line in zone B
- They score a point by stopping the ball on the end line, under control
- Both teams are limited to three touches in their defensive zone but are allowed free play in their attacking zone

## Switching Games
- Once players have experienced the three different games, the coach randomly calls out a number and the players quickly switch to that game, as in exercises 186 to 192
- The coach should change the games quickly in order to make players think

# Exercise 194

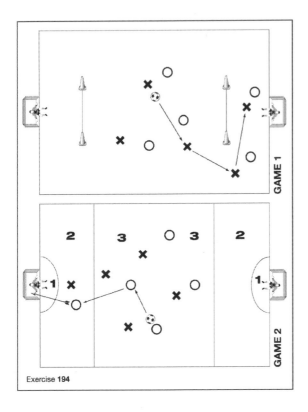

Exercise 194

**Equipment:** 16 cones, 4 goals, disks, balls, set of bibs  **No of players:** 24

**Time:** 20 min                                              **Pitch size:** 40m x 25m x 2

## Game One
- Play 5 v 5 + two goalkeepers
- Two x 20 metre lines are marked out with cones, 20 metres from each goal line, as in the diagram
- Neither team can pass the ball across these lines
- This will force teams to play wide, both in defence and attack
- A free kick is awarded to the opposition for any pass across either line

## Game Two
- Play 5 v 5 + two goalkeepers
- A 10-metre semi-circle is marked out in front of each goal
- A 35-metre line is marked out 15 metres from each goal line, as in the diagram
- Teams win a point if they score from a shot inside the semi-circle, two points if they score from a shot inside the 35-metre zone and three points if they score from a shot outside the 35-metre zone

## Switching Games
- Once players have experienced both games, the teams switch pitches on the instructions of the coach, as in games 186 to 193
- The coach should change the games quickly, in order to make players think

# Exercise 195

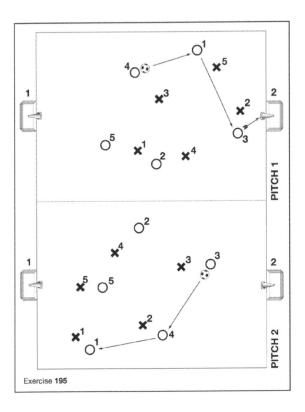

Exercise 195

**Equipment:** 6 cones, balls, 4 goals and set of bibs  **No of players:** 20

**Time:** 20 min                                    **Pitch size:** 40m x 25m x 2

## The Game
- The group of 20 players are divided into four teams, with two teams wearing bibs
- Play two games of 5 v 5. The teams play on adjacent pitches, as in the diagram
- The players are numbered from 1 to 5
- On pitch one O's attack goal 2 and defend goal 1
- On pitch two O's attack goal 1 and defend goal 2
- Teams score by striking a cone placed in the middle of the goal

## Switching Games
- Once a rhythm has been established, the coach randomly calls out a number or numbers (eg 1 and 4)
- The players with these numbers leave their game and sprint across to the other game on the adjacent field
- Those players whose numbers were not called out, continue with their game
- How quickly can players adapt to the new game?
- The coach should keep calling out different numbers, in order to make players think

## Exercise 196

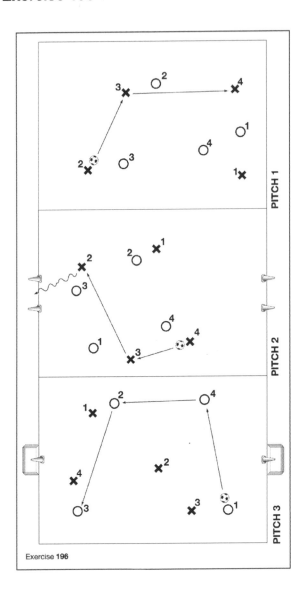

Exercise 196

**Equipment:** 14 cones, 2 goals, set of bibs, and balls   **No of players:** 24

**Time:** 20 min                    **Pitch size:** 30m x 25m x 3

## The Game
- The group of 24 players are divided into six teams, with three teams wearing bibs
- The teams play three different games on three adjacent pitches
- The players are numbered from 1 to 4

## Game One
On pitch one, teams play 'keep ball', with both teams aiming to keep possession

## Game Two
- On pitch two, teams attack and defend a 15m goal, marked out with four cones
- The aim is to stop the ball on the line, between the cones and under control

## Game Three
- On pitch three, teams attack and defend a goal
- They score by striking a cone placed in the middle of each goal

## Switching Games
- Once the players have experienced all three games, the coach randomly calls out a number or numbers (e.g 2 and 3)
- The players whose numbers are called out sprint to the next game
- Therefore the players whose numbers are called on pitch one, sprint to pitch two, those on pitch two sprint to pitch three and those on pitch three sprint to pitch one
- The players whose numbers are not called out continue with their game
- How quickly can players adapt to the new game?
- In order to make players think, the coach should keep calling out new numbers

**Chapter 15**

# Conclusion = Having Fun

*'In training, the soccer scrimmage form must be used most of the time, just as in street football.'*
**Rinus Michels**, FIFA Coach of the Century

It is easy to forget that while children are being prepared for life in the adult world, they are still children, with a whole range of varying needs. It must be recognised that they have different requirements, so if a person is coaching children, they must have the knowledge to do things differently than if they were working with adults or elite soccer players. It is therefore essential to raise the standards of coach education, so that children's coaches are trained specialists in the field of youth sport and have a far better understanding of child development and the science of teaching. They have the responsibility to create an environment that allows both physical and mental development. The early years are crucial in establishing good habits, creative thinking, physical attributes of agility, strength and speed, for example, and a player who has learned and developed through purposeful play.

Certainly coach education has got to change quickly if the demands of the 21st century are to be met. At present, much of coach education is based on previous generations. Unfortunately most coaching today does not recognise that children are reflective of the society they grow up in, and that society has changed dramatically in the last 30 years.

Today's youth are gravitating away from the natural world and the opportunities to explore and play, in favour of sedentary indoor activities. Children of all ages and socio-economic backgrounds have greater opportunity to be inactive more than ever before through computers and television than from self-directed, imaginative play. Studies conducted with the Kaiser Family Foundation, released in 2006, found that one third of children from six months to six years of age grew up in households where TV was on all or most of the day. In one generation children have stopped challenging their senses and so the brain is getting wasted in terms of its capacity to grow via the motor sensory system.  It is therefore the job of the coach to stimulate movement and all the senses whenever possible. This will only happen if the coach designs a programme which:

• Ensures the children are having fun
• Makes them feel they have some level of influence over what happens

in the training sessions as discussed in the development of ownership of decisions made in problem solving tasks

- Improves their skills, which enables them to feel they can be successful
- Provides a relationship with others; sport is the great socialising opportunity
- Is child-directed and the rewards come from within the individual. This will ensure they want to get better
- Uses appropriate and effective teaching styles.

Stuart Brown, Founder of the National Institute for Play, refers to play as something that "shapes the brain, opens the imagination and invigorates the soul". It develops children's physical, mental and creative abilities. It helps them practise eye:hand and eye:foot coordination and develop the physical agility to run, jump, walk and balance. Through play a child learns the social etiquette of taking turns whilst developing an awareness of other people's views and feelings and the consequences of their actions. The child learns how to problem solve whilst developing curiosity and intellect. To a child, life is play - and play, very importantly, should be fun. These are the natural consequences of spontaneous play and all of these learnt without a coach!

With this in mind, it is essential to engage young players when they start to play football. It is not the coach's job to instruct, but to stimulate the imagination so success is achieved when the child finds passion and excitement in what he is doing. This is the time for play, exploration and fun, not drills and constant practice. The reference to rigid, organised sessions highlights how all this passion and excitement can be lost.

From an adult's point of view, work without play is boring, and demotivating. People cannot rise to the highest level in their job if they do not enjoy what they are doing - grinding out the work is not enough. Without a sense of fun or play people cannot stick to any discipline long enough to master it. Players only reach the highest level in sport because they are driven by enjoyment, passion and competition.

When Alan Ball retired from playing, I asked him what it was like to have such a long and successful career. Without hesitation he replied, "I was lucky because all I ever wanted to do was play professional football. Football was my passion so work became my passion – every day was like being the proverbial kid in the sweet shop." To Alan, work was play and so he would go back most afternoons and put in extra practice with anybody who shared the same passion as him. Alan loved what he was doing, so work simply became play. Perhaps that's why, at his peak, he was arguably the best one-touch player in the world.

It is therefore no coincidence that the world's top players are products of a free play environment. Brazil, Argentina and more recently Uruguay are the world's greatest exporters of professional footballers and the most envied in terms of the richness of talent. These are closely followed by many of the African nations. As Dr Tom Turner explained clearly in his article 'Training Muscle Memory', in the free play environment in which most of these players grow up, there are no lines, referees, linesmen, coaches, laps, drills or lectures. Similarly, there are no cones, shuttle runs, hill runs, hurdles, ladders or poles. Instead, there are games with randomly selected teams of varying ages and abilities, uneven playing surfaces and in some cases not even the correct footwear. Players left to their own devices slowly learn skills over time. One situation is never the same as the next and if a dribble or pass fails, then that player has the opportunity to try that skill over and over again. We have all learned through mistakes and the lessons learnt save us from repeating those mistakes. Coaches should encourage that risky, challenging environment in their coaching. When we were younger, we found the right way through exploration and through a few falls - the equivalent of climbing trees. Difficult playing surfaces such as sand or rutted ground enhance touch and proprioception.

It is more difficult to promote free play in European countries, so the coach must be clever and vary the conditions, particularly in youth soccer (5 to 10 age group). This will allow the learner to develop generalised motor programmes, enabling him to cope with a variety of similar but different situations. It's for this reason that variable and random practices are better for skill learning, as they recreate street football in an unstructured type of training and this promotes learning from mistakes. Players need to play the game and discover what works and what doesn't in open, not closed, situations. This will mean the coach adopting a more "hands off" approach to players' education, although the make-up of exercise and games will be vital.

Are our coaching styles and win-at-all-costs philosophy having a negative effect on the creative mind of young players and forcing them into a structured environment from a young age? This seems to be the case, so it is now essential to recreate playful and experimental practice in order to allow children to develop self-expression, imagination and invention. Variable and random practice, in the form of small-sided games, must be at the heart of all our training sessions. If this format is followed, players will become more familiar with simple patterns of play and perception within game play. Also, from a young age they will start to develop visual acuity (ability to track passes from distance), depth perception and visual memory, along with better anticipation and decision-making skills. It is essential that we develop players for the future who are able to improvise and respond whatever the situation!

Developing game-playing skills is critical for effective soccer performance. During game play the player becomes responsible for assessing game needs and then responding with the appropriate decisions and skills. However, for too long the coach has had the responsibility for assessing game problems and then trying to find the solutions. It is time to move away from this formula and use teaching styles which make it player-centred rather than coach-centred when learning the game. To achieve this, it is essential to use teaching styles which give players autonomy, both in games and training.

Technical, tactical, physical and social skills (the four corners) all affect game performance and players are able to develop these better if they are given the freedom and opportunity to make choices and develop their own decision-making. As has been stated earlier, it is not being suggested that there is only one teaching style; there are various teaching styles that can be used alone or in combination to increase a player's autonomy and ability to make sound decisions when practising the game.

Decision-making is players' ability to solve practical problems within the game, so we have to provide them with more problem-solving opportunities in realistic game situations. Teaching players to become better decision-makers will involve empowering them to take control of their own performance. The coach therefore has to implement various strategies which will enable each player to enhance their decision-making abilities. He must guide players through the process of solving problems and establish an environment in which players share responsibility for their own learning and that of the team.

Coaches should be encouraged to use a more player-centred approach to learning, so that their role becomes more facilitator than instructor. We must therefore use a method of coaching which enables players to take ownership of their own learning, development and decision-making. The question and answer method or guided discovery method would be the optimum way of achieving this as both encourage players to think critically and allow them time to solve problems and formulate their own ideas. If players are unable to do this, then the coach needs to guide them to the right decision, not just tell them.

Young players need to work in an open framework where variable and random practice are the basis for training. Small-sided games should therefore always be at the heart of the practice. Young players need to be involved in the game, either on the ball where they can show their prowess or off the ball where they are learning the signals of the game according to the actions of their team mates or opponents. A player cannot learn these skills by standing in line or performing drills. When players learnt in the street, they were always practising a version of the real game and were developing visual search patterns, awareness and anticipation skills. The coach can use the 'street' method of learning and enhance it by using coaching methods that set the team play framework but allow the players to make the decisions within that framework.

Coaching is not about just feeding information into players but enabling them to learn. If knowledge is merely presented by experts to non-experts and decisions are made for the latter, then learning becomes minimal. The knowledge, understanding and decision-making that players learn and apply will make all the difference between success and failure. Our style of coaching must enable players to take ownership of their learning, but how many coaches would be prepared to allow this?

The programmes created must meet the developmental needs of the players and stimulate them to excel and reach their full potential. We believe the games in this book will help players achieve these aims and enable them to be responsible for their own learning. However, coaches must be aware that the game of soccer is evolving constantly and what is valid today could be out of date tomorrow. It is therefore essential to produce coaches who can adapt to these ever-changing demands in order for us to stay competitive and cultivate players who are inventive, skilful, highly motivated and able to think for themselves.

*"It surprises me how our culture can destroy curiosity in the most curious of all animals – human beings"*
**Paul Maclean**

# Bibliography

1000 ejercicios y juegos de Futbol Base. Walter Butcher and Bernard Bruggman. Hispano Europea (2003)

America Idle. Mary Collins. Capital Books (2009)

America Heart Association (no date) cited in Hannaford C. (1995). Smart Moves. Why learning is not all in your head. Great Ocean Publishers. Alexander.NC

An introduction to Sports Coaching. From Science to Theory and Practice. Routledge: London Jones L.J., Hughes M & Kingston K (2009)

Assessment of secondary school students' decision-making and game-play ability in soccer. Minna Blomquist, Tomi Vantinen and Pekka Luhtanen, Physical Education and Sports Pedagogy Vol 10, No 2 (June 2005)

Athletic Development. Vern Gambetta. Human Kinetics (2007)

Athleticism. Vern Gambetta. Strength and Conditioning. Sports Coach

Children Moving. Graham Holt / Hale Parker. Sixth Edition. McGraw-Hill (2004)

Children and Sports Training   Jozef Drabik, Ph.D. Stadion (1996)

Coaching Children. Sports Coach. Vol 23 No 4 (2001)

Development of Movement Coordination in Children. Geert Savelsburgh, Keith Davids, John van der Kamp and Simon J Bennett. Routledge Taylor and Francis Group (2003)

Developing Game Intelligence in Soccer. Horst Wein. Reedswain (2004)

Elements of Psychology. Krech D, Crutchfield R.S. New York (1982)

Ensenza Del Futbol En Las Escuelas Deportives De Iniciacion. Rafael Moreno del Castillo and Jose Alfonso Morcillo Losa. Gymnos Editorial Deportiva

Exuberant Animal. The Power of Health, Play and Joyful Movement. Frank Forencich. Author House (2006)
Factors influencing physiological responses to small-sided games. Ermanno Rampinini, Franco M Impellizzeri, Carlo Castagna, Grant Abt, Karim Chamari, Aldo Sassi, Samuele M Marcora. Journal of Sport Sciences (April 2002)

Fundamentals of Human Neuropsychology. Bryan Kolb, Ian Q Whishaw, New York (1985)

Game Sense. Coaching Children. Sports Coach (1996)

Game Situation Training for Soccer. Wayne Harrison. Reedswain (2005)

Game Vision in Soccer. Critchell, Bosma and Granger. Reedswain (2009)

Hekkesluiters 1, Senso-Motorishe Ontwikkeling. Kephat N Rotterdam (1981)
Implicit Learning; an alternative approach to instruction. Damian Farrow.
Skill acquisition, Australian Institute of Sport and Sports Coach

Influence of a Hybrid Sport Education - Teaching Games for Understanding unit on
one teacher and his students. Physical Education and Sports Pedagogy. 11(1) pp.
1 - 27

Last Child in the Woods. Richard Louv. Atlantic Books (2010)

Learning Disabilities and Brain Function. Geddes W.H New York (1985)

Learning to Teach Physical Education. Prentice Hall London
Tinning R. Kirk D. & Evans J. (1993)

Let's play 3 v 3! Large sided games often turn into small sided games with
everybody else standing around. So why not start small? Jack Kern and Paul
Calleja, Journal of Physical Education, Recreation and Dance (August 2008)

Motor Learning and Control. Magill R.A. New York (2011)

Neuropsychology, A Clinical Approach. Walsh K.W. New York (1978)

Perception. Robert Sekular / Randolf Blake. McGraw-Hill (1994)

Perceptual and Cognitive Expertise in Sport. Mark Williams. The Psychologist Vol
15 No 8 2002

Play. Stuart Brown. Penguin Group. (2010)

Reading the Play in Team Sports. Damian Farrow Australian Institute of Sport.
Sports Coach Vol 27 No 3 (2004)

Revisit Game Sense. Alan Launder. Sports Coach

Smart Moves. Why learning is not all in your head. Alexander: Great Ocean
Publishers
Montague A cited in Hannaford (1995)

Smart Moves. Why learning is not all in your head. Great Ocean Publishers
Roosevelt T cited in Hannaford C (1995)

Smart Moves. Why learning is not all in your head. Great River Books. Alexander NC. Hannaford (2005)

Soccer Coaching 10-15 year olds. Stefano Bonaccorso. Reedswain (2001)

Spark! How exercise will improve the performance of your brain. John Ratey and Eric Hagerman. Quercus (2008)

Sports Coaching Cultures: From Practice to Theory. Routledge: London McGeechan cited in Jones R, Armour K & Potrac P (2004)

Sports Expertise: From theory to practice. Bruce Abernethy School of Human Movement Studies University of Queensland. (Paper presented 2005)

Talking a Good Game. John Cartwright and Roger Wilkinson Premier Skills. Wolverhampton (2001)
Teaching the Skills of Soccer. Jose Segura Rius. Reedswain. (2001)

Teaching Physical Education (5th edition). Mosston M, & Ashworth S (2002) Merrell Publishing Co. Columbus, Ohio

The body has a mind of its own. Sandra Blakeslee and Matthew Blakeslee. Random House (2007)

The Right Brain. R Blakeslee. Macmillan Press (1980)

The Spanish Soccer Coaching Bible. Youth and Club. Laureano Ruiz. Reedswain (2002)

The Spanish Soccer Coaching Bible. High School and College. Laureano Ruiz. Reedswain (2002)

The Talent Code. Daniel Coyle. Random House (2009)

Training for speed of thought and speed of play. Dave Eliot. New Hampshire Soccer Coaches Association

Understanding Children's Development. Smith P.K, Cowie H, Blades M. Blackwell Publishing (2003)

Warm Ups for Soccer – A Dynamic Approach, Mick Critchell. Reedswain (2002)

Who's Who of the Brain. Kenneth Nunn, Tanya Hanstock, Brian Lask. London (2008)

## Articles from the internet

Advantage of playing small-sided games. Glenn Buckley. Director of Coaching, New York State

Benefits of playing 4 v 4 soccer in a diamond shape. Fran Kulas. Director of Coaching and Player Development

Circuit Model Hallamshire Presentation 31.8.07. Martin Diggle

Functional training in soccer / livestrong.com. Multi-axial movements for soccer.

Importance of triangular shape in soccer. Soccer Shape, Size and Space. www.bettersoccermorefun.com

Lines of Interaction. Sam Snow, US Youth Soccer National Staff Instructor

Right and left brain in soccer. The street soccer coach overview. Darren Laver (2010)

Training Muscle Memory-Soccer Fitness. Dr Tom Turner. Director of Coaching, Ohio Youth Soccer Association (2010)

## Articles from magazines

The Manchester United 4 V 4 Pilot Scheme for Under 9's: Part II – The Analysis. Fenoglio, R. (2003). Insight - The Football Association Coaches Association Magazine. 6(4), 21-24.

# About the Authors

## Mick Critchell

Following a successful career as a Head of Physical Education and Head of Year in secondary schools, Mick has focussed on football coaching. He works with players at all levels - from "grass roots" to professional. He has been coach and fitness adviser to Farnborough Town FC and Basingstoke Town FC, coach at Portsmouth FC School of Excellence and coach educator for Hampshire FA and Surrey FA. He has worked as an in-service trainer for the Premier League Football Academies and for both the Swedish FA and the Polish FA, and is currently a consultant for Fulham FC.

He is also the author of three best-selling books: "300 Innovative Soccer Drills for Total Player Development", "Warm Ups for Soccer - A Dynamic Approach" and "Game Vision in Soccer", and co-presenter of the video: "Going for Goal". In addition, he is a director at The Football Garage, an approved centre for 1st 4 Sport.

## Bo Bosma

Bo is a Dutch national who qualified in 1987 as a clinical psychologist and a neuro-psychologist at the State University of Utrecht. After qualifying she took a fellowship at the University of Antwerp and continued to work in a children's observation centre.

In 1990 she started work in Dublin as a neuro-psychologist, specialising in memory disorders.After moving to England, her children started playing football. This gave her the opportunity to analyse football training in community and academy settings. It soon became clear that there was no particular training structure that took into account children's development. Frustrated with the observations, she met with Mick Critchell who introduced her to more challenging and creative ways of training. From here, her interest in cognitive sport psychology developed.

## Richard Cheetham MSc

After completing a Masters degree in sport science at Brunel University, Richard travelled to New Zealand where he lectured in sports coaching as well as strength and conditioning. He was fitness coach for Massey University Rugby in Palmerston North and the provincial Sevens team, Manawatu. Success with both these teams led him to work with the New Zealand Academy of Sport, the NZRFU and the Olympic White Water Kayaking team. Since his return to the UK in 2004, he has been a lecturer at the University of Winchester where he now holds the position of Senior Lecturer in Sports Coaching. As an RFU Coach Educator, he has been able to develop both his own coaching and that of others in a way that addresses the need to provide the best teaching and teaching environment for players. Richard has completed the Atacama Ultra desert marathon in 2010 and still coaches his local club, Basingstoke RFC. He feels that the completion of this book will be the start of encouraging others to develop an engaging, challenging and yet rewarding coaching style and philosophy. The results will be refreshing for all involved.

## Mark Hurst

Mark is currently Head of Physical Education, Director of the Fitness Centre and Head Coach of the Boys Varsity Soccer team at TASIS, The American School in England. He took his FA Prelim qualification in 1977, whilst studying at St Mary's College, University of London, and found it completely at odds with his education studies. This stimulated a lifelong study into coaching and teaching young players. Influenced by John Cartwright and Dario Gradi, Mark worked and studied the methodology of young player coaching at Ajax and Bayern Munich, and has been working with Villarreal since the inception of their famed academy. In England he has worked for Southampton and Fulham, and has campaigned for 30 years for a change in the structure of youth soccer in England. In 2002 he started an experiment with Sandhurst Town Saracens U7 team using the approach promoted in this book; they became known as the 'Spanish team in Berkshire'. He has presented at conferences in Switzerland, Tunisia, Belgium and Finland and in 2012 will become the Chair of the Physical Education Committee for the European Council for International Schools.

We need to develop players with game intelligence, who can play in different systems and positions and adapt to the ever changing demands of the modern game. Game intelligence is an intelligence built almost entirely on experience and determined by the type of practice that players get. Euro 2012 has highlighted the need to take a different approach to working with young players and this book leads the way in encouraging the thought and understanding required to develop the next generation of footballers.

**Kit Symons**

Fulham Development Squad Manager
Wales Assistant Manager

Find other Reedswain soccer coaching titles at:
**www.reedswainsoccer.com**